W9-DDO-576

Property of the
Grand Valley State
University Libraries

INEPTITUDE, CONFORMITY, AND OBFUSCATION

WITHDRAWN

WITHDRAWN

INEPTITUDE, CONFORMITY, AND OBFUSCATION

The Fraud of Teacher Evaluation in the Public Schools

Richard J. Giordano

ROWMAN & LITTLEFIELD
Lanham • Boulder • New York • London

Published by Rowman & Littlefield
An imprint of The Rowman & Littlefield Publishing Group, Inc.
4501 Forbes Boulevard, Suite 200, Lanham, Maryland 20706
www.rowman.com

Unit A, Whitacre Mews, 26-34 Stannary Street, London SE11 4AB

Copyright © 2019 by Richard J. Giordano

All rights reserved. No part of this book may be reproduced in any form or by
any electronic or mechanical means, including information storage and retriev-
al systems, without written permission from the publisher, except by a reviewer
who may quote passages in a review.

British Library Cataloguing in Publication Information Available

Library of Congress Cataloging-in-Publication Data

Giordano, Richard J.
Ineptitude, conformity, and obfuscation : the fraud of teacher evaluation in the public schools
ISBN 9781475841596 (cloth)
ISBN 9781475841602 (paper)
ISBN 9781475841619 (electronic)

™ The paper used in this publication meets the minimum requirements of
American National Standard for Information Sciences Permanence of Paper
for Printed Library Materials, ANSI/NISO Z39.48-1992.

Printed in the United States of America

DEDICATION
This book is dedicated to the memory of "Uncle Joe"
A common man
An uncommonly kind man

Joseph Giordano
1914-2004

CONTENTS

PREFACE

Having left classroom teaching to begin a master's program in preparation to become a school principal, I found the coursework required for the degree to be absent much solid content, content I had assumed would be present when I began the work.

Several years later, having been a high school principal for several years, I had taken all the courses and had been awarded all the degrees, culminating with a doctoral degree in education. But notwithstanding degree status, solid content remained missing.

With all these degrees attained, I felt deserving of the comment made by a character in one of writer Bert Vincent's homespun stories. In the story, a city lawyer finishes his vocabulary-rich commentary on a matter of law, one more confusing that enlightening to those in the courtroom. The opposing lawyer, questioning the veracity of what the young man said, drawls a sighs and says, "Ain't he high lernt?"[1] I felt something like that, highly schooled but not very highly educated.

What I knew was that, through all of the classes taken, very little real subject material had been provided. There was no truly applicable content (real stuff!) in all those education classes I'd taken. Nothing came remotely close to being content-substantive and thereby applicable to real-life situations in either the classroom or school—and this was particularly so for my task of evaluating the teachers teaching their subjects in my school.

As an undergraduate student with a biology minor, I took classes in botany, zoology, physiology, anatomy, and others of what were called the hard sciences. I learned some real stuff! I came away actually knowing something! But now, having gone through all the graduate classes and having achieved a doctoral degree in education, I came away with a very different, and disconcerting, thought. "Piled higher and deeper" was perhaps more than just a humorous slur about degrees in "education"! Had I just become dumber, by degree?

But I was not alone in this. Many of my principal colleagues also spoke, mostly in subdued tones, about the "education" classes they had taken in their undergraduate days as virtually worthless. And while it seemed tacitly understood to be nearly the same in their graduate schooling, few made similar comments about their graduate degree coursework—that which qualified them for their status as principals, or even as the higher-up positions in the administrative educational bureaucracies to which some aspired.

Now, having "been there, done that" as a high school principal for many years, I can see that there's a lot more to the state of our current public education system failures than just the university-provided coursework that teachers and administrators engage. What is more apparent now is that there exists little leadership or accountability in public schools today. And the interrelationship of these two is apparent: The dearth of leadership from school principals and superintendents, that group from which one might expect it to come, is what allows for the absence of accountability in the production of a quality product: well-educated students.

At the root of the failure to provide high-quality teaching to students is the failure of school principals to know if quality teaching is being done. In short, what is promoted as "teacher evaluation" to the public is a fraud. As will become clear, there are more players in this veritable perfect storm of inadequacy than just school superintendents and building principals . . . many more! All of these conform in presenting a false narrative to the public—that being about teacher evaluations. That narrative is fraudulent!

Ineptitude, Conformity, and Obfuscation: The Fraud of Teacher Evaluation in the Public Schools may seem to be a rude act of finger-pointing. But as Rudy Giuliani, the former mayor of New York City, said, "Choosing one word over another is an important act."[2]

Thus, these words are chosen carefully to discriminate clearly what is on-the-ground happening in public schools today. "Ineptitude" is most likely inadvertent, not purposeful. However, "conformity" and "obfuscation" would appear to be largely volitional—purposeful. "Fraud," be it inadvertent or otherwise, is the result of the enactment of these three. The word is herein chosen to portray reality: **Fraud**.

Constructive fraud: In law, a fraud that is involved in an act or contract that, though not originating in any actual or fraudulent design, has a tendency to deceive or mislead other persons, to violate public or private confidence, to impair or injure the public interests.[3]

While the above is a legal definition, the process of teacher evaluation is commonly thought to be nonlegalistic in nature. However, given that public schools are government schools that are paid for by the legal taxation of the populations they serve, with teachers and administrators acting as the schools' legal agents via state certification standards, schools are inherently legal entities. Therefore, the misrepresentation (fraud) of an act carried out by the schools, in this case the teacher evaluation process, is injurious to the public's interest, that interest being their young people's realization of a quality educational experience.

It is not within the province of this writer's knowledge or intent that the teacher evaluation process herein described is done with malicious intent by those individuals and/or organizations involved. The process taking place today in teacher evaluation may be largely the result of what has been an organic evolutionary set of circumstances, events that have played out since the creation of the head teacher, later to become the school principal, in days long gone by. But the observable fact that virtually all participants in the process either fail or refuse to identify why it does not, and cannot, achieve its intended ends is not evolutionary. That part is purposeful.

Many participants, individuals and organizations, allow this fraud to continue: boards of education, professional educational organizations, teacher unions, superintendents, principals, teachers, prominent writers in the field of education, and university professors within colleges of education. All these, joined together by choice or circumstance, form what I define as the education coterie of public education. To be discussed in greater detail later, suffice it to say that all of these coalesce in advancing, supporting, and maintaining programs and processes that are inappropriate for, and sometimes harmful to, children in the public schools. Teacher evaluation, the topic of this book, is but one of those impacted by their involvement.

In addressing the matter of teacher evaluation, the intricacies and nuanced variations of evaluation instruments will not be part of the discussion. Part of what is wrong with teacher evaluation today is that too many in education focus on the minutiae, that which is inherent in the instrumentation. Elaborately developed "rubrics," largely designed and promoted by those bureaucratic inhabitants of the education coterie, routinely result in the micromanagement of teachers and how they teach. These are put-offs to both teachers and the principals who are coerced into using them!

The principles of sound teaching are not so difficult as to demand such micro-scrutiny. Some of these, such as the ability to communicate clearly and salesmanship, will be addressed. Above all, the matter of independent thinking and the promotion of common-sense approaches to teaching are paramount. The herd mentality, sometimes called the procession of the lemmings, keeps school principals, and other so-called leaders in public education, ensconced within processes that do not work, and will not work.

As will be shown, leadership in public education is virtually nonexistent today. The systems in place in public schools, those currently garnering the approval of the education coterie, do not allow for real leadership—the kind of leadership that leads without concern for consensus-based approval. In many ways, being a school principal today requires the kind of mindset described by an ancient Greek philosopher, Aristotle: "To lead an orchestra, you must turn your back on the crowd."[4]

But it is not parents on whom principals should turn their backs. Many have been doing too much of that recently! It is the educational bureaucracy, the education coterie, from which school leaders, mainly principals, should break ranks. This will be difficult! As will be seen, it is coterie group-think that prevails upon principals to silently abide the demands of groups such as LGBT activists and other such groups that would have schools become societal petri dishes for their radical social agendas. In these, the wishes of parents are shunted aside in deference to the aberrant behaviors advocated by the activists, and enabled by the education coterie.

This book is not about blaming any person or group of persons. It is about confronting a problem in teacher evaluation systems used in the public schools, one that leaders in public education have ignored. What is presented here represents what is happening in the public schools today, not what most principals and their superintendent bosses say is happening. It's about that pesky elephant in the room, the pachyderm that the education coterie promulgates. It's about the fraud of teacher evaluation!

ACKNOWLEDGMENTS

As a high school principal for over twenty years, but not having worked in public education for several years, I wanted to be sure that what I would be reporting about teacher evaluation was accurate. In order to get a boots-on-the-ground view of current practices, I consulted with several people currently involved in various positions in public education: high school principal, high school assistant principal, middle school principal, high school dean of students, district director of professional development, director of human resources, university professor of education, director of educator effectiveness, administrator/state department of education, director of state high school athletics association, and district director of secondary education.

I wish to thank these educators for their willingness to engage in conversations with me about the work they do. Their insights have been valuable in helping me formulate *my* thoughts about what is currently the state of teacher evaluation in the public schools. While by no means a *statistically significant* sampling assessment of teacher evaluation practices, I believe that those with whom I spoke provided a fair and balanced assessment of the most common practice in today's schools.

My intent in seeking the views of those I spoke with was to determine if what I *thought* was happening in the evaluation of teacher performance today was, *in fact*, happening. What I found, from my conversations with these people, was that the practices that principals employ for the evaluation of their teachers have remained essentially unchanged since the time I left public education.

Recognizing that some might be uneasy offering their candid responses, I assured each person with whom I spoke that no information in my work would allow a future reader to identify anyone by either position or name. In keeping with this arrangement, the following list identifies the school districts or associated public school agencies wherein I conducted interviews:

Boulder Valley Public Schools, Boulder, Colorado
Weld SD #6, Greeley-Evans, Greeley, Colorado
Jefferson County Public Schools, Golden, Colorado
Denver Public Schools, Denver, Colorado
Aurora Public Schools, Aurora, Colorado
Indiana University, Bloomington, Indiana
Colorado Department of Education, Denver, Colorado
Gilpin County Public Schools, Black Hawk, Colorado
Vigo County School District, Terre Haute, Indiana
South Vermillion County School Corporation, Linton, Indiana
Indiana State University, Terre Haute, Indiana
Cedar City School District, Cedar City, Utah
St. George Public Schools, St. George, Utah
Henderson Public Schools, Henderson, Nevada
Las Vegas Public Schools, Las Vegas, Nevada
West Bend Public Schools, West Bend, Wisconsin
Michigan State University, East Lansing, Michigan
Colorado High School Activities Association, Denver, Colorado

Once again, I express my sincere appreciation to Dr. Tom Koerner, vice president and publisher for education issues with Rowman & Littlefield Publishers. As was the case when I worked with Tom in writing my first book, he afforded me wide latitude to go about my work. His insights and suggestions have been invaluable to me, and I am grateful to him for the help he has given me. A fellow south-sider from Chicago of many years past, I have appreciated his erudite professionalism. More so, I have enjoyed his friendship.

Finally, I want to say how *very* much I appreciate the assistance that Dottie Eichhorn gave me throughout this project . . . from start to finish! She read *every* page, kindly giving me her thoughts on both what I'd said and how I'd said it. I am certain that, due to her sharp eye for detail, she saved the editorial staff at Rowman & Littlefield a lot of editing . . . and me the necessary follow-up. She has been the *best* of the many blessings I have experienced in writing this book!

INTRODUCTION

Often you may hear a person express concern about young people today, saying something like "What's wrong with these kids today? They don't seem like they know anything!" Aside from the exasperation expressed, this question is quite insightful. It suggests that young kids don't know anything, and things are facts! The underlying sentiment here is that the kids are not being taught subject-matter content in school. If you associate this question with the education rank of the United States as compared to other nations based upon student testing, you'll glimpse why this is an appropriate question to ask. Compared to all other nations tested, the United States doesn't make it into the top ten![1]

If you were to ask people in your neighborhood if their children have good teachers, you'd likely get a near reflexive "Yes!" But if you followed up by asking how they knew that their teachers were good, you might hear the sound of silence . . . or perhaps one of two responses: "Well, my kids get good grades, so the teachers must be good" or "My kids aren't doing very well, so those teachers aren't doing their jobs." But how would anyone know? That's what this book is about.

This book is about answering the parents who may ask their school officials, "Are my child's teachers doing a good job teaching, and how can I know this?" School officials should be able to respond by saying, "Yes, your child's teachers are doing a good job of teaching your children! We know this because our teachers' abilities are evaluated by well-trained professionals. From these evaluations we know that they are teaching correct subject-matter content, and that they are teaching it effectively." School officials should be able to assure parents that these two basic tenets of good teaching are both present; accurate subject-matter content is being delivered to students, and the process of delivering it is effective. It's the product and the process, interacting together, that make for good teaching. But can today's school officials give parents this assurance?

In the interest of openness and transparency, you should know that the theme of this book is that school officials today cannot give parents this assurance. What you will be reading herein is that the teacher evaluation processes in today's schools cannot assure parents that either the right content is being taught, or that what is taught is being taught effectively. You will also learn why this is so. This book is about teacher evaluation in public schools, a process that is not up to the task of doing that which it purports to do: to assure parents that good teaching is taking place in their schools.

In getting at the "nuts and bolts" of why teacher evaluations are inadequate, envision a civil courtroom prosecution, one in which "teacher evaluation" is on trial. In this trial, what is being persecuted is "Fraud." In this prosecution, you might also consider some "codefendant" behaviors to be acting in the support and perpetuation of the defendant, Fraud. These are "ineptitude, conformity, and obfuscation."

In order to get at the facts of this case, several people (as participant-members of groups) will be described for the roles they play. School superintendents, school principals, teachers, parents, school boards, and state boards of education are but a few that will be examined. But none is being charged, as an individual or as a group member, with any misdeed. The words of Leonardo da Vinci describe best what is intended by scrutinizing these participating people and groups: "Learn how to see. Realize that everything connects to everything else."[2]

It is the interconnectivity of all these that redounds to today's ineffective teacher evaluation outcome. However, regardless of this ineffectiveness, at no time should you think that the arguments made herein make the claim that good teaching is not taking place today. This is not intended. While there are poor teachers in the public schools, there are also lots of excellent teachers, teaching solid content and teaching it very well! The only charge leveled herein is that there is no good way to know, one way or the other.

In the end, you will decide this question: "Is the teacher evaluation process used in your schools today effective or ineffective in assuring you that the teachers are doing a good job of teaching your children?" And it can be difficult to answer this kind of question. You may feel as though you are in a kind of vacuum, one wherein you can't envision another alternative to the one you are being asked to judge. For this reason, another way to evaluate teachers is provided for your consideration, intended to be a better one. Now you can compare.

As was said in the beginning, the intention of this book is to explain a process taking place in the public schools, a very important one. It is one that parents do not know very much about, if anything at all, but they should! If what you read in the following pages convinces you that some changes should be made in your school, then the purpose of this book will have been accomplished. What you do next is up to you, but at least you will be able to know! After all, it's about education, it's about knowing!

1

THE WAY WE WERE

A Brief History of Schooling and Teacher Evaluation

As is true of most things in life, what we do today reflects what we did in the past. If a means of governance for populations of people tried in the past did not work, the people found a better way. In America, the founders rejected old orders of top-down governance and put in place the democratic republic form of government that we enjoy to this day. Education in the United States has followed this same pathway, with older forms giving way to what are *perceived* to be better ways of doing things. But are the new ways better?

In the 1600s, 1700s, and into the mid-1800s, America's teachers taught their classes in the absence of any kind of formal supervision or evaluation. Largely of a religious orientation, church pastors would involve themselves to be sure that a Christian education was being taught, but the teachers were largely left to their own devices.

Until the late 1800s, teachers continued to teach in largely unsupervised classrooms. These predominantly male teachers typically taught *all* the first eight grades in one-room schoolhouses wherein students were not separated by grades. There were no school principals at the time, so any form of teacher evaluation was left to the individual perceptions of parents and others in the community.

Today, some form of teacher evaluation is in place in every public school in the country. Teacher evaluation's origins and evolution, through the decades of the nation's history, provide an insight into why we have what we have in the public schools today.

EARLY HISTORY: CHRISTIAN SCHOOLING

Notwithstanding the pronouncements of some people today, the historical record shows clearly that the United States of America was founded as a Christian nation. Nowhere is this displayed more clearly than in the early colonial period of history. During this time the schools aggressively promoted the various denominations of the Christian faith.

Prior to the advent of state school systems in the middle decades of the nineteenth century, the rich religious diversity that characterized overwhelmingly Protestant colonial and early national America was manifested in an equally rich diversity of Protestant schools. Throughout these years, Lutherans, Quakers, Presbyterians, Moravians, German and Dutch Reformed, Baptists, Methodists, and Anglicans established elementary schools and academies. Even the so-called town schools of colonial New England and the quasi-public district schools and charity schools of the early 1880s were de facto Protestant schools.[1]

Unlike American public schools in the 21st century, religion played a central role in the schools in the colonial period of the 1600s. Schools were agents of the church with the intended purpose of advancing the cause of God, as community members believed that cause to be. Unlike public schools today, often attacked by antireligion activists for manifesting even a *hint* of religiosity, these early schools enjoyed broad-based community support for their religious focus. Their goals for teaching the children were about the present and future welfare of the child, and their textbook spoke to this purpose:

> It may surprise many to know that the Bible was truly the first textbook. The New Haven Code of 1655 required that children be made "able duly to read the Scriptures" and in some competent measure to understand the main principles of Christian Religion necessary for salvation.[2]

The schooling in colonial times was not intended to prepare its students for any particular job, or with any particular set of skills for making a living. The driving idea of the time, in addition to its focus on God, was to form good and right-thinking citizens. There was an emphasis on preparing some students for their future university attendance, but the universities were vastly different at that time: "Harvard had been formed in 1636 with a grant from the Massachusetts Bay Colony as a training ground for Calvinist ministers. Thus, grammar schools were needed to prepare Harvard with well-prepared students."[3] Notwithstanding the very few who went on to higher education, the main focus of early schooling was to prepare young children to live productively God-driven lives.

The culture of the 1600s colonial period, and well into the 1700s, was manifest as powerfully religious both in the public square and in the schools. The influence of a strong cultural religiosity of that time is further evidenced by the founding of its early institutions of higher education. One hundred and six of the first one hundred eight colleges in America's early history were founded on the Christian faith: Harvard College (1636), William and Mary (1691), Yale University (1701), Princeton (1746), and the University of Pennsylvania (1751) are but a few examples of these.[4] Given these universities' foundational charters, it is little wonder that the schools throughout the communities had a similarly religious focus.

As will be seen, the religious nature of schools changed in the mid-1800s. But at the turn of the new century, religion still was the bulwark of public education. John Adams, the second president of the newly established United States of America, made this clear: "Our Constitution was made only for a moral and religious people. It is wholly inadequate to the government of any other."[5] While history does not record how many people were present when these words were spoken, or how many might have read them or heard them subsequently quoted by others, President Adams voiced the prevailing sentiment of the time.

STUDENTS AND THEIR TEACHERS: WHO WENT . . . WHO TAUGHT THEM?

Unlike today, school attendance was neither required nor the rule in the early history of the United States. In the early 1600s most children had no place to go as a common meeting place for learning, largely schooled at home by their parents. This began to change with the passage of a law that began formalized schooling in the country: "In 1647, Massachusetts passed the 'Old Deluder Satan Law,' requiring every town of 50 households to appoint and pay a teacher of reading and writing, and every town of 100 households provide a Latin Grammar School."[6] Notwithstanding the establishment of these schools, many parents continued to school their children at home.

In the 1700s, common schools came into being in communities wherein students were taught in one room and by one teacher. These schools were not uniformly attended by all the children in communities of such populations because they were not free. "Parents paid tuition, provided housing for the school teacher, or contributed other commodities in exchange for their children being *allowed* to attend these schools."[7] As some parents could not afford tuition, the cost of housing and feeding a teacher, or the other *commodities* required, school attendance remained an option for children, and so not all children went to school.

The 1800s ushered in a change in the way students were taught. Prior to this time, no educational requirements or preparatory formal training for teachers was prerequisite for becoming a teacher. Those thought to have been good learners in their own school days were selected as the community's schoolteachers. Considered to be intellectually sound via their own schooling achievements, they were selected to teach school after they themselves left school.

These early teachers, perhaps overwhelmed by the numbers of students and varied subjects they were expected to teach, initiated a unique system of handling both. They initiated the monitorial system in their classes, an approach to teaching that would evolve over time into university colleges of education today.

The monitorial system, also called the Lancasterian system, was the teaching system practiced most extensively in the 19th century, in which the older or better scholars taught the younger or weaker pupils. In the system as promoted by the English educator Joseph Lancaster, the superior students learned their lessons from the adult teacher in charge of the school and then transmitted their knowledge to the inferior students.

Parents of the monitors, however, objected to the learning time their children were losing, even though many of the monitors were paid a small weekly sum. It was found that some training of the monitors was necessary, and in about 1840 the movement began that replaced monitors with "pupil-teachers"; that is, boys and girls who, at the age of thirteen, were apprenticed for a period of five years, during which they learned the art of teaching while continuing their education under the head teacher of an elementary school. Some such programs developed into normal schools and training colleges, in which professional and academic education could be continued after the apprenticeship was completed.[8]

While perhaps an unintended consequence, the evolutionary sequence from *monitor* to *pupil-teacher* and then to attendance at a normal school provided the first criteria-based format for the evaluation of a teacher's performance. "By the 1930's most formal public normal schools evolved into teachers colleges, and by the 1950's they had become departments or schools of education within universities."[9] All these training institutions taught a curriculum containing a systematized "how-to-teach" pedagogy. As such, they provided the very first behavioral means of assessing teaching performance by way of asserting a set of established, commonly accepted standards.

Almost simultaneously, school began to change in another substantial way, beginning in the mid-1800s with the advent of the *public common* school system. The new public common school systems of this era, the mid-1850s in the north and 1870s in the south, did not maintain a strong religious motif. This shift in emphasis, from the religious to the secular, along with a more formalized approach to teacher training, marked a dramatic philosophical change of direction for the nation's public schools. Both what was taught, and how it was to be taught, underwent a change that was not to be reversed from that time forward.

Another landmark change occurred in the mid-1850s. School attendance shifted from a matter of parental choice to a governmental requirement. Compulsory school attendance became a matter of law when Massachusetts passed the very first of these laws in 1852. The spread of these laws was neither instantaneous nor uniform across the developing country.

Mississippi was the last state to enact a compulsory education law in 1917. And these laws were not to be ignored. They carried stiff penalties for those who did: "Parents who refused to send their children to school were fined and (in some cases) stripped of their parental rights, and their children apprenticed to others."[10]

The face of public education had irrevocably changed in the country. Parents were now obligated to submit to the state for the schooling of their children and whatever the state deemed appropriate in that endeavor. And for those who continued to desire that their children's schooling should retain a strong *Christian* orientation, it was not to get any better.

CHRISTIAN SCHOOLS TO SECULAR SCHOOLS: WHAT WAS THE DIFFERENCE?

Beginning in the mid-1850s, in addition to newly enacted compulsory attendance laws, the school systems that had served communities earlier in the century began to undergo a dramatic change in orientation. A new thinking began to emerge wherein religiously founded and oriented schools were now thought to be "un-American and divisive."[11]

A new approach sought to supplant religious instruction with a more secularized form of teaching, teaching wherein a focus on the Bible gave way to secular-oriented subject matter. In short, the *three Rs curriculum* (reading, writing, and arithmetic) previously taught to facilitate religious-growth aims now changed to focus on the academic subject content itself—content not oriented nor intended to serve a biblical focus.

The church pastors who previously watched over the teachers and their content instruction, making sure that biblical content was taught correctly, gave way to citizens, sometimes a small committee of a few parents, now residing in less religiously homogeneous communities. And as this transition from the religious to the secular progressed, a slippage in content knowledge—*knowing*—began to evolve in these new public schools.

The citizens, themselves not necessarily schooled in the subjects taught, did not necessarily possess the knowledge of the subjects to judge whether or not they were being taught correctly. Compared to their predecessors, ministers and pastors who were versed in the Bible content being taught, they did not have the same ability to *know* the content in the new subject areas.

It would be inaccurate to say that the ministers of an earlier day were all experts in one uniformly accepted Bible theology within a community. As is true today, the various denominations (Baptist, Roman Catholic, Lutheran, etc.) had nuanced interpretations of biblical chapter and verse. However, all agreed upon the basic message, manifested by the Ten Commandments in the Christian Bible. The fundamental truth of content was not vague, and *knowing* this content armed the ministers to determine if incorrect content was being taught.

Ministers of this era also scrutinized the *way* their teachers taught their Bible lessons: the *process* of their teaching. Appropriate treatment of the students, good speaking ability, exceptionally strong classroom discipline, rigorous testing, and other aspects of teachers were all part of ministers' interests. But these issues were not the center of gravity of the ministers' focus. While teachers' presentations were considerations in their performance reviews, the accuracy of content taught remained the centerpiece of their scrutiny. They wanted and expected to see prolific and accurate biblical instruction in the classrooms they visited.

WHAT WERE THEY WATCHING?: IT WAS ABOUT *FOCUS*

As schools became progressively more complex due to the increasing number of teachers in them as well as more subjects being taught, community members began to recognize a need for some form of *onsite* management in each school, to allow for attention beyond what they could provide as citizen-supervisors. As a result, the somewhat informally-arrived-at position of *head teacher* came into being.

Beyond his or her teaching duties, the person appointed head teacher oversaw a variety of administrative tasks in the building: scheduling activities and ordering textbooks as well as other routine organizational tasks. Typically, those thought to be the very best teachers were appointed to this position.

When created, the duties of the head teacher largely involved clerical and minor administrative functions. But these changed over time. As the size and educational scope of schools increased, the head-teacher position eventually evolved into the position of school principal. The most significant aspect of this change was that this new position did not include teaching responsibilities.

The principal was now a full-time school administrator, responsible for running the entire school operation. Subject-matter expertise, previously required for a teaching position, was usually a prerequisite in order to be a principal, but it became more a qualifier than a necessity for performing the duties of the principal position.

Clearly, the head-teacher supervisors of 1800s schools were not proficient in all the subjects taught. Like today, they were proficient in the three Rs, the mainstay subjects commonly taught in elementary grades, or specialized in one or perhaps two subject areas at the higher grade levels. As a result, other than their routine administrative duties, head teachers did not provide any form of evaluation of their colleagues.

When the position of school principal came into being in the mid-1870s, the supervisory functions expanded to include student-related matters, but other duties of the position remained much the same.

Although the principal's job was to coordinate the different classrooms of the graded school into "one system of governance," that job was originally quite limited in scope and centered primarily on tasks of maintaining order and discipline.

There was virtually no conception of the principal's role as a community or intellectual leader; the principal served as a functional manager only, with specific responsibilities only for addressing student registration and discipline. [12]

So far, this has been a historical recounting of the past, from the early colonial period to the final years of the 1800s: days of long ago when head teachers watched their teacher colleagues deliver their lessons. While possessing no formal training, these early-stage school principals essentially saw to it that the teachers were teaching what was to be taught. Even with the creation of the position of school principal, the teacher evaluation function did not significantly change in that principals remained largely managers.

But in the 1900s, a larger educational issue would arise, one that would raise the teacher evaluation function higher to become more important in the eyes of educators and the general public as well.

WHERE ARE WE GOING?:
IT'S *THIS* WAY . . . NO, IT'S *THIS* WAY!

In the early part of the 1900s, now that compulsory education of the nation's youth was the law of the land, the question of what *purpose* education should serve was asked with greater frequency. The question might have been commonly phrased, "So now that it's the law, what's it for?!"

While many offered their opinions, center stage in providing answers were two people: philosopher and educator John Dewey and mechanical engineer Frederick Wilson Taylor. These two offered completely different approaches to the *function* of education. Their differences centered on two questions: (1) What is the purpose of education? and (2) What is to be taught to achieve that purpose?

Dewey held that education's sole purpose was to prepare young people for effective participation in society. He saw survival of the country's democracy as dependent upon that singular function. Young people needed to be informed so as to be active and vital participants in a country's existent social order and ultimately progress toward an even better order. "Education is social progress; education is growth; education is not preparation for life but is life itself."[13]

Dewey's approach was hands-on, experience-based, and engaged the students in their learning activities. They were no longer merely recipients of dispensed information, but active participants in engaging it.

The starting place in Dewey's philosophy and educational theory is the world of everyday life. Unlike many philosophers, Dewey did not search beyond the realm of ordinary experience to find some more fundamental and enduring reality. For Dewey, the everyday world of common *experience* was all the reality that man had access to or needed. For Dewey, learning was primarily an activity that arises from the personal *experience* of grappling with a problem. This concept of learning implied a theory of education far different from the dominant school practice of his day, when students passively received information that had been packaged and predigested by teachers and textbooks.[14]

The role of education, through Dewey's eyes, was to provide young people with a wide variety of educational experiences, experiences wherein they would develop their unique abilities to solve problems encountered in everyday life. The integration of seemingly unrelated bits and pieces of information, and arriving at a cohesive understanding of how they all fit together, was his goal. He was a pragmatist, a believer in the words of Leonardo da Vinci: "Learn how to see. Realize that everything connects to everything else."[15] Through his approach, young people would not only become self-sufficient, but also contributing members of the social order, through their understanding of how all the pieces interrelated.

Frederick Taylor took a different approach, one that had a narrow focus on workers in the early 1900s. His concern was industrial productivity and how product quality and output could be increased by workers. He envisioned a system of education whose aim it was to improve both.

Taylor's views were popular with people at the time because the industrial culture was changing, and he saw the direction in which it was moving. Parents too began to raise questions as to whether or not the schools were keeping pace, asking if their schools were teaching the things their children would need to succeed. They demanded that their schools reform to meet the changing times.

One of the primary concerns of many Americans was that society was changing rapidly during the 1900s and the nation's schools were failing to prepare their students for the many new challenges that lay ahead. The most important cultural shift was the economy's transformation. Large industrial corporations were gradually replacing agriculture and small manufacturing, which had once been the most powerful sectors of the economy.[16]

With cultural change afoot, Taylor was looking for new ways to get better results, and in what ways the workers might be schooled to produce them. He saw workers as the tools to achieve that end. In his scheme, the education the worker received should be determined by the end he was to produce: "no great man can (with the old system of personal management) hope to compete with *a number of ordinary men who have been properly organized so as to efficiently cooperate.*"[17] (emphasis mine)

The idea that the school curriculum should turn out young people who were prepared to do specific jobs proved persuasive. In his book *Public School Administration* (1929), Ellwood Cubberley advanced Taylor's argument regarding the purpose of schooling: "Our schools are, in a sense, factories in which the raw products (children) are to be shaped and fashioned into products to meet the various demands of life. The specifications for manufacturing come from the demands of twentieth-century civilization and it is the business of the school to build its pupils according to the specifications laid down."[18]

Others who followed Cubberley's thinking suggested that the measurement of teaching practices in schools was also an important part of the process, because it determined whether or not educational goals were being achieved. In this regard, teachers became more prominently featured for their roles in bringing about expected outcomes.

A CHANGE OF FOCUS:
FROM WHAT'S RIGHT FOR THE JOB TO WHAT'S RIGHT FOR THE TEACHER

The approaches advocated by both Dewey and Taylor, commonly referenced as "scientific," were soon to become colored by yet another new *wrinkle* in the fabric of public education, one wherein the *teacher's welfare* became of paramount importance:

> The period immediately after World War II began with a swing away from the scientific approach to schooling. Rather than describing supervisory processes in terms of raw materials and products, the literature began to focus on the teacher as an individual. Emphasis was placed on not only assisting the teacher to develop his or her unique skills, but also tending to his or her emotional needs.[19]

John Dewey was often said to be the father of *progressive education.* And while the term "progressive" is largely associated today with the political left, public education in the mid-1900s took a turn in a similar direction. The teacher's emotional needs became a factor in supervision and classroom performance evaluations. From this point onward, the focus of teacher evaluation would be influenced, and significantly so, by psychologists, social scientists, and others whose primary focus was the welfare of the teachers.

The welfare of teachers would become a high-priority issue for the two largest teachers' unions in the country, the National Education Association (founded in 1857) and the American Federation of Teachers (founded in 1916). Both were ostensibly founded to advance the cause of public education, but the trend toward a more refined focus on the welfare of their members would increase in importance as time passed. Along with societal changes taking place after World War I wherein labor unions demanded better working conditions for their workers, the teachers' unions made similar demands for their workers.

With the passage of a "collective bargaining" law in Wisconsin in 1959, the first of its kind in the country, the issue of *process* now became part of the education dialogue regarding the treatment of teachers, and its influence extended into the ways in which its members were to be evaluated.

In schools across the country there began to emerge the belief that *cooperation* between the principal and teacher was important in the evaluation process. The term "stakeholders" was now heard with increasing frequency, circumscribing teachers' new roles in their evaluations. They were no longer merely acted-upon entities within a process, but critically important parts of the process.

A SHIFT IN VIEWPOINT: BIOLOGY APPLIED TO TEACHER EVALUATION

In the late 1950s, clinical supervision became the dominant paradigm employed by school principals in their evaluations of teachers. As mentioned, no longer did principals assume 100 percent management and control of the teacher evaluation process. Now they collaborated with their teachers in cooperatively arriving at an assessment of the teachers' work. Robert Goldhammer's five-point model depicted teacher evaluation as parallel to a biological principle, a principle applied in evaluation systems in hospitals at the time: "The process involved a purposeful, *symbiotic* relationship between practitioner and resident, where observation and discussion drove the parties to higher levels of growth and effectiveness."[20]

Symbiosis is a biological principal wherein two living organisms owe their lives to the actions of each other, each unable to survive absent the participation of the other. An example of symbiosis is a complex form of plant life, the lichen. The lichen is not *one* organism, but *two* organisms living together as one. Half the organism is made up of algae, and the other of fungus. The fungus breaks down rock on which the organism lives so that minerals can be made into food, simple sugars, by the algae. The fungus, unable to produce its own food owing to its lack of chlorophyll, is nourished by the food produced by the algae. Each survives and thrives through the actions of the other.

Employing this new *symbiotic* approach, principals continued to sit in teachers' classrooms to watch them teach. But they now incorporated teachers' input as an integral part of their evaluation format. Principals now held meetings with their teachers, both before and following classroom visitations, establishing teachers' collaboration and cooperation in their evaluations as the foundation for the process. And while Goldhammer's model for teacher evaluation fell out of favor, this new collaborative aspect lived on. It grew more in impact as the next model for teacher evaluation emerged onto the educational scene.

CRITERIA AND PROGRESS: WHAT TO LOOK FOR . . . HOW TO LOOK

Since the beginning, when school people sought to evaluate teachers and their teaching, a variety of methods have been tried, only to be subsequently abandoned. One trait that all had in common was that, as their means of gathering information, they had a person sitting in a classroom, watching. Typically, this person was the school principal. Perhaps the first approach to teacher evaluation to be applied nationally was the Madeline Hunter mastery learning model.[21]

As stated, the clinical supervision model for teacher evaluation arose out of the 1950s and gained increasing application across school districts in the 1960s and 1970s. Superintendents of the time thought this highly *structured* approach was the right approach to teacher evaluation. Now, while incorporating much of the clinical supervision evaluation precepts, mastery learning became the lingua franca for the evaluation of teacher performance.

Mastery learning became a virtual wave sweeping across the country to become the most widely accepted model for teacher evaluation. But not all were 100 percent on board with this one-size-fits-all approach.

As was the case with clinical supervision, the Hunter model contained seven *precisely defined* criteria to be applied in evaluating teaching, even more finite than its precursor: (1) learning objective, (2) anticipatory set, (3) lesson objectives, (4) input, (5) checking understanding, (6) guided practice, and (7) independent study.

Principals scrutinized teachers' teaching for the presence of these seven criteria in the classrooms, now designated to be the absolute markers/measures of good teaching. Now principals and their teachers spoke in terms reflecting the seven mastery learning categories of excellence, employing a plethora of the now-in-vogue terms and phrases. While mastery learning enjoyed broad appeal and usage, some began to speak to some of its deficiencies:

> The Hunter Model has a number of advantages, and an equal number of disadvantages. For instance, it is a great drill and practice model. The model is an excellent one for content or processes that benefit from lots of repetition. However, without considerable thought, revision, and artful manipulation, the model's repetitive structure is not appropriate for open-ended learning experiences, discovery learning sessions, or exploratory educational experiences, especially ones requiring divergent thinking skills, creative problem solving, or higher thinking skills.[22]

And "Hunter's mechanistic and simplistic model does not improve the quality of education because it stifles teacher and student thinking."[23]

Notwithstanding these criticisms, mastery learning continued to be considered the *gold standard* for teacher evaluation. As such, it remained the most common means used by principals for the evaluation of their teachers. Albeit with changes in terminology and logistical and structural categorizations, it remains the strategy employed in most school districts in the country today. While other nuanced approaches have come and gone, most of the principles of mastery learning have remained the most widely applied principles in use to the present time.

A DRAMATIC EVENT:
CHANGE AFOOT . . . BUT PERHAPS NOT!

Perhaps no other event in the history of public education made as big an impact in media and educational circles as did the *A Nation at Risk* report of 1983.[24] Commissioned by President Ronald Reagan through his Commission on Excellence in Education, a committee was formed to study the state of public education in the United States. It included eighteen members from the private, government, and education sectors. This report, a hallmark in the history of public education, clearly defined the problem for the nation's schools in its introductory remarks:

> If an unfriendly power had attempted to impose on America the mediocre educational performance that exists today, we would well have viewed it as an act of war. As it stands, we have allowed this to happen to ourselves. We have even squandered the gains in student achievement made in the wake of the Sputnik challenge. Moreover, we have dismantled essential support systems which helped make those gains possible. We have, in effect, been committing an act of unthinking, unilateral educational disarmament. [25]

The report sent shock waves through the educational community in the United States, prompting school districts to hurriedly engage new programs and processes to portray to the public, and themselves, that the report's message was being taken very seriously. The report's findings covered a broad range of failures in the public schools and suggested ways that these could be resolved. Needless to say, there was a flurry of activity in public schools to incorporate the report's recommendations to show that its message was being heeded. But as much activity as was generated at the time, the results of new approaches were not destined to be long-lasting.

Since *A Nation at Risk* made its debut in the spring of 1983, various measures of educational reform efforts that followed have continued to yield inconsistent answers to the question of whether or not the schools are better today than they were prior to the issuance of the report. However, there seems to be an overall agreement that the results of these efforts have not brought about the changes that the report stated as necessary. Both the effects and longevity of changes made are still subject to question among school people and citizens alike.

In a report issued by the American Institute for Research, the results do not seem to show that changes, those to make a positive impact, have been either effective or long-lasting. Jennifer O'Day, a contributing writer for the report, states what is perhaps the most pervasive reason for the report's not having resulted in lasting change:

Why did we not realize the turnaround "over the next several years," as the report's authors thought possible? One factor, often noted, may be interest-group and partisan political battles over particular reform recommendations or strategies. Americans may consistently agree that "education is extremely important to one's future success" and that it should rank among the nation's top funding priorities (as the report's authors observed), but we are less likely to all agree on how our educational systems should achieve the goals we individually hold dear.[26]

UP TO DATE:
WHERE WE ARE TODAY

If the history of public education displays anything as a central theme, it is that change has been ever present—sometimes even *dramatic* change! Certainly the establishment of the first public schools, along with enactment of mandatory attendance laws that were to follow, was upsetting to community members of the time.

Today's public-school parents are no doubt similarly upset by some of the practices and programs that have found their way into their public schools. And the political framework that is now so prevalent in the public schools, referenced by Jennifer O'Day above, makes for a more visible debate on virtually *any* issue involving public education.

In the early 1900s, the public schools became the subject of some of the influential writers of the time, such as John Dewey. As time passed, more writers became commentators on the state of public education, on both its pluses and minuses. And while seventeen years have passed since his opinions were first published, the assessment of public education offered by Martin Gross may bring us up to the present time in this historical review, at least as pertains to the *problems* in public education.

In his book, *The Conspiracy of Ignorance*, Gross presents his synoptic assessment of the state of education in modern America.[27] It is his comprehensive assessment of the state of public education just before the dawn of the 21st century. In detailing the breadth of problem areas in public education, Gross puts forth his views via his Indictment of the Educational Establishment. In his indictment, he identifies *nineteen* areas of failure in the public schools. Among these, he discourses on how teachers are trained, licensed, motivated, and organized but makes only a fleeting mention of teacher evaluation, and this reference just relates to *when* and not *how* teacher evaluations are conducted.

This then brings us to our current place in the history of public education in America. With a brief recounting of the history of schooling and teacher evaluation, it becomes more apparent how public education, and the function of teacher evaluation, developed from the beginnings of schooling in America. The next section, chapter 2, will endeavor to explain what is happening in the public schools today, and specifically what is happening in the realm of teacher evaluation. The story will be not be about what was happening in public schools in the 17th, 18th, 19th, or 20th centuries, but what is happening *right now*, in the 21st century.

A VISITOR'S ASSESSMENT: FROM THE PAST TO A VIEW FORWARD

Alexis de Tocqueville came to America with his lawyer-friend Gustav de Beaumont in 1831. His purpose for his voyage from his home country, France, was to study the prisons in America.

> From Sing-Sing Prison to the Michigan woods, from New Orleans to the White House, Tocqueville and Beaumont traveled for nine months by steamboat, by stagecoach, on horseback and in canoes, visiting America's penitentiaries and quite a bit in between. In Pennsylvania, Tocqueville spent a week interviewing every prisoner in the Eastern State Penitentiary. In Washington D.C., he called on President Andrew Jackson during visiting hours and exchanged pleasantries.[28]

What Tocqueville didn't plan on learning on his trip was just how *educated* the general population was in America, and the value that this high degree of enlightenment had upon maintaining its way of life:

> It cannot be doubted that, in the United States, the instruction of the people powerfully contributes to the support of a democratic republic; and such must always be the case, I believe, where instruction which awakens the understanding is not separated from *moral edu-*

cation which amends the heart. But I by no means exaggerate this benefit, and I am still further from thinking, as so many people do think in Europe, that men can be instantaneously made citizens by teaching them to read and write. True information is mainly derived from experience; and if the Americans had not been gradually accustomed to govern themselves, their book-learning would not assist them much at the present day.[29] (emphasis mine)

WHAT'S NEXT?:
WHERE WE ARE . . . A BASIS FOR WHERE WE SHOULD BE

In the next chapter, the current state of teacher evaluation in the public schools becomes the focus. This will be addressed before any suggestions for change are suggested. There is a reason for this ordering of events. In order to propose the notion that teacher evaluation needs to be improved, a foundational reason for the existence of teacher evaluation must first be addressed. The first question should be, Is *any* form of evaluation needed? In short, if nothing is wrong with what teachers are teaching and doing, why is there a need for *any* form of evaluation?

On first glance, given Tocqueville's words of wisdom (to the extent we value them today as such), it is apparent that the "moral education which amends the heart" is absent, from both the design and practice of public education in America today. Nowhere in 21st-century education (in approved curricula, instructional practice, or extracurricular activities) is found that which Tocqueville referenced as *absolutely necessities* in order for Americans to keep their freedoms. Search for these essentials in any public school . . . you will not find them!

Tocqueville's assertion of the need for a moral educational construct is but one of *many* things that are in need of serious scrutiny in the public schools today. In short, there's a *lot* going in the public schools that is not what should be going on! And teachers play a large and increasingly active role in what's going on. In large measure, they are intimately involved with the initiation and practice of what's going on, both in the subjects they teach, how they choose to teach them, and in the general social structure and prevailing culture of the school.

Now, before getting into how teachers are evaluated, it is fitting to have a brief review of *what* is taking place in the schools, beyond *just* what is happening in teachers' classroom instruction. The roles they play in what goes on beyond their classroom influence, in addition to their teaching performance inside their classrooms, has not traditionally been a focus in their overall performance evaluations. It should be!

The next chapter will deal with a variety of activities in the public schools in which teachers play significant roles. These are things that are *wrong* with the public schools today, and also things to which teachers have routinely remained unattached in terms of their performance evaluations. With this more comprehensive view of a teacher's activities within the school, a far more comprehensive format for teachers' evaluations may then be addressed.

2

TEACHER CLASSROOM-EVALUATION: IS *THAT* ALL THERE IS?!

What Flies Under the Radar

If you were to look into any workplace, an automobile manufacturing plant for example, you would expect to find people divided into two categories. You'd expect to see people actively engaged in the jobs to be done, the *workers*, and you'd see people making sure that the jobs were being done properly—the supervisors.

The supervisors evaluate the workers, assuring that the work is done in accord with predetermined expectations. *Any* task done by the worker, one that influences the quality of the product being produced, is subject to the scrutiny of the supervisor. For example, in a job that requires a worker to perform twelve distinct operations, the supervisor scrutinizes each distinct operation to assure that the job is completed properly. No task can be overlooked if a quality outcome is to be achieved.

In public education, one might expect that this straightforward practice similarly might be in place . . . but one would be wrong! Continuing with the manufacturing paradigm, the quality of educational experiences provided to students is subject to a *plethora* of operations conducted within the school. Each of these is owed supervision to assure that a quality product results: a well-educated student. But in fact, the workers largely responsible for this product, the teachers in a school-workplace, are supervised in only *one* aspect of their work by their supervisors, the principals. They are supervised, evaluated, almost exclusively in only their *subject-matter* teaching performance.

In the culture of a public school, much takes place in the *subject-centered* classroom, aside from subject-matter instruction. All of it coalesces to inform the quality of education received by the student. And just as with the manufacturing example, supervisors, typically school principals, are watching the teachers perform their work.

But the principals are not watching *all* the *operations* performed by the teachers. They are missing *much* of what the teachers are doing, things that have a substantial and profound impact upon the quality of the product being produced: well-educated students.

In this chapter, the things that happen in the public schools, things typically *not* addressed in teacher evaluation processes, are the topic. *So* much happens in schools today, things that leave parents and community members alike scratching their heads in emotionally charged wonderment and crying out: "Have the teachers lost their minds? What ever happened to common sense?!"

Historically, public schools have been places wherein the values of the community have been reinforced and promulgated. And while cultural values change over time, these values have traditionally been founded in well-grounded moral and ethical principles, and some scientifically established facts that serve to reinforce them.

As was stated in chapter 1, the Christian tenets of the Ten Commandments were central in the early public schools, with strong emphasis on commandments five through ten. Highly important was the concept of "truth," as it was defined both via social interactivity within the community and its intersection with scientific definitions available at the time.

But truth, reinforced by science, has been redefined in the public schools today. What was widely recognized as "common-sense" education in the past, as exemplified by John Dewey and Frederick Wilson Taylor (chapter 1), is now an endangered-species form of thinking. Teachers still instruct their students in what to *know* regarding accurate subject-matter knowledge; e.g., here are the anatomical differences between a reptile and an amphibian. But now some teachers also *indoctrinate* their students in *how and what* to think, increasingly about far-reaching social-agenda issues. And unlike teaching biological fact, what teachers are teaching here is anything but truthfully "settled science."

But why focus on teachers? The reason is that the promotion of social-agenda issues, largely politically liberal, is not the work of the secretaries, custodians, or the lunchroom ladies. The idea that *teachers* are substantively responsible should come as no surprise to you! It is *they* who have contributed mightily to public schools becoming the veritable social-experimentation petri dishes that they have become. And as will be seen, notwithstanding a plethora of state-sanctioned strategies and teacher evaluation rubrics, public schools' teacher evaluation systems do not address *any* of these matters.

It must be noted that principals, the ostensible "leaders" in their buildings, remain responsible for all that takes place in their buildings. The role of the principal as the leader of his/her school, in this matter and others, will be addressed later. For now, suffice it to say that the leadership role of principals has been greatly curtailed to the extent that principals are no longer in a substantive decision-making mode for much of what transpires in their buildings. A few all-too-common examples of what the schools now incorporate into their curricula will display an educational system that has lost sight of its historically founded purpose: educating children.

TEACHER, MAY I GO TO THE BATHROOM? OF COURSE, JOHN. OOPS . . . I MEAN *JOAN!*

In a Colorado school district (thirty thousand students K-12), the board of education has seen fit to empower its teachers to make decisions critical to their children's welfare, ones that can effectively serve to controvert parental wishes. The district's Gender Support Plan[1] also functions in supporting the *miseducation* of its students, in two ways.

First, the implementation of the plan appears to disallow parents their appropriate, and legally founded, decision-making role regarding their children. Second, it allows teachers to engage in advocacy-teaching, a classroom approach that promotes a program that is questionable at its best and dangerous at its worst. Both are accomplished to the detriment of the students.

The issue is "transgenderism." This school district has implemented a curriculum wherein students are encouraged and enabled in making decisions as to the nature of their sexual identities. In a word, it's about a boy deciding, autonomously, that he wants to be a girl, or a girl wanting to be a boy. These *children* say that they want to "identify" as the sex opposite the one of their birth. And that is *all* that is deemed necessary for this school district to begin aggressively supporting, and advocating for, the student's decision.

But what does this have to do with teachers teaching their *subjects*, or how they are evaluated for doing so? In the academic subjects, English, mathematics, and foreign languages for example, the effect of the district's formal policy position is unremarkable. But in one area, health education, the impact is both profound and detrimental regarding the health, as well as the education, of the students.

In this Colorado school district, a policy is in place (File: AC-ES)[2] that reveals the school district's agenda, the one that the district demands its teachers embrace. One portion of this document appears to show that parents are removed from a *decision-making* role regarding the "gender identifications" of their children. In the section titled "Parent-Guardian Involvement," the following questions reference the district's address to the matter of sexual identity: "Are guardian(s) of this student supportive of their child's gender status? Yes/No. If not, what considerations must be accounted for in implementing this plan?"

If the answer to this question were "No," one might assume that the school district would revisit the appropriateness of going forward with its "plan" to enable the student in making a gender-identity change. But it appears that one would be wrong in this assumption! The wording of this section implies that the district will move forward with its plan, notwithstanding the views of the parents. Reading further in this district's plan, other "correct-response" protocols are listed:

How will a teacher/staff member respond to questions about the student's gender form?

Name to be used when referring to the student.

How will instances be handled in which the incorrect name or pronoun are used?

How are some other ways the school needs to anticipate information about this student's preferred name and gender marker potentially being compromised? How will these be handled?

What training(s) will the school engage in to build capacity for working with gender-expansive students?[3]

As noted previously, John Dewey was perhaps the most significant educational reformer of the 20th century. His words may best describe what happens to students when activist advocacy groups influence what happens to children in the public schools:

> For in spite of itself, any movement that thinks and acts in terms of an 'ism becomes so involved in reaction against other 'isms that it is unwittingly controlled by them. For it then forms its principles by reaction against them instead of a comprehensive survey of actual needs, problems, and possibilities. [4]

For whatever reason, teachers in this school district appear to be in a *reactive* mode; they are teaching students to fear and avoid what *might* occur regarding other students, rather than the proactive role of teaching what *should* be occurring for other students. They are "ism-reactive," per Dewey's comments. In this district, teachers advance a dangerous strategy of miseducation, teaching their students that there is only *one way* to think!

TEACHERS DISTORTING REALITY:
ONE VOICE IN THE ROOM → ONE-WAY THINKING

In the K-12 health curriculum in this school district, teachers bring in speakers that are on the district's "approved" list to speak to their classes. Most of the people the health teachers bring into their classrooms present fact-based educational information, information that most people would consider reasonable: healthy eating habits, injury prevention, avoidance of drug use, etc. But some that are brought in promote beliefs and behaviors that are more akin to political agendas than fact-based information.

In this school district, these "approved-list" speakers are members of advocacy groups. As such, they approach students as activists, not educators. Greater diversity, an oft-employed buzzword in public education today and particularly in this school district, is typically the guise under which they advance their advocacy for their issues. Their topics are about LGBTQI (lesbian, gay, bisexual, and transgendered, questioning, intersex) issues, increasingly focusing on transgenderism and "gender identity" issues.

As most people recognize, the issues of "gender identity" are far from the status of *settled science*. Unlike what this school district allows its students to hear about this topic, there is another side to the story—what a news commentator used to refer to as *The Rest of the Story*.[5] The commentator was Paul Harvey, well known by radio listeners in the 1950s.

The stories Mr. Harvey told on his national syndicated radio show always revealed what went unreported, the so-called backstory in today's news terminology, and they were always revealing and enlightening. And while Mr. Harvey would most accurately be described as a news *commentator* in stating his unique opinions, another prominent newsman of the era dealt in what is today called *hard news*: Walter Cronkite.

Like Mr. Harvey, Walter Cronkite dedicated himself to reporting the truth . . . *all* of the truth. His beliefs about reporting the news are summed up in one short statement: "In seeking truth you have to get both sides of a story."[6] The characteristic these two newsmen shared was that they did not conflate opinion with truth. Each drew a distinct line between the two. This line is blurred, or absent, in the LGBTQI presentations given in the classrooms in the school district activities here described.

The absence of a dissenting point of view, one differing from the pro-LGBTQI agenda brought in by the speakers, is an example of one side of the story being told, but only one side! More about this later. For now, suffice it to say that this slanted-teaching strategy *flies under the radar* of teacher performance evaluations. This behavior, by the teachers who choose to bring these advocacy speakers into their classrooms, goes unaddressed in their performance evaluations. In this school district, as is likely in many other districts, this kind of advocacy-teaching has become acceptable "professional" behavior.

WHY ARE THEY TEACHING THIS STUFF?!
TEACHERS TEACHING THAT WHICH THEY KNOW NOT

As stated earlier, the matter of *choosing* one's sexual identity, an identity differing from one's biological birth identity, is far afield from "settled science." The fact that there remain two sides to this issue is a crucial distinction that renders its *promotion* by teachers educationally unsound. In a word, it is "miseducation."

Many recognized experts in the sciences understand that there remain a host of issues relating to sexual identity that are not fully understood. Much remains unknown. But what *is* known does not support the skewed information that teachers allow to be presented in their classrooms, from either common-sense or scientific fact standpoints. As will be seen later, school administrators, those evaluating teachers' performances, pay substantial attention to *how* teachers teach, but are in near lockstep conformity in paying little or no attention to *what* they teach.

In the field of neuroethics, Drs. James J. Giordano and Bert Gordijn concur with other scientists in stating that transgenderism is a phenomenon not yet fully understood. They state that complexity of hormonal chemistry interactivity within the developing brain during gestation is critical regarding the determination of sexual identity, both normal and aberrant. And while substantial strides have been made in understanding these phenomena, there remain far more questions asked than answered: "whether endocrine disruptors, i.e. chemicals in the environment, for instance from industry, influence sexual differentiation of the brain is an important question for the future (Swaab 2007)"[7] and "there is a vast array of factors that may lead to gender problems."[8]

The phenomena that the public schools treat as naturally occurring human phenomena are referenced by Drs. Giordano and Gordijn as "gender problems." One might ask why "gender problems" are treated as normally occurring human phenomena by the public schools, rather than as biological anomalies—those possibly caused by harmful chemical agents acting on the gestational development of human beings. But rather, these are being taught as commonplace normalcy in public school classrooms. And as stated, they go unchallenged by any opposing point of view.

> The American College of Pediatricians issued a statement condemning gender reclassification in children by stating that transgenderism in children amounts to child abuse. The American College of Pediatricians urges *educators* and legislators to reject all policies that condition children to accept as normal a life of chemical and surgical impersonation of the opposite sex.[9] (emphasis mine)

Walt Heyer has firsthand knowledge of what a full embrace of LGBT education efforts can bring to children. As a former transgendered youth, he warns parents that what is currently taking place in their schools is dangerous:

> Those who design these programs probably believe that they are offering hope to children who may feel different, flawed, or unlovable. They believe that if they affirm children's LGBT identities as something positive, something that makes up the core of who they are, the children will fare better.
>
> This is not the case. No matter what well intentioned teachers and administrators believe, these programs ultimately entail an agenda that hurts kids. The messages these programs send do nothing to combat the tragically high suicide rates among the LGBT community. Data indicate that kids are actually put at risk when schools encourage them to identify themselves as gay or transgender at an early age. For each year children delay labeling themselves as LGBT, their suicide rate risk is reduced by 20 percent.
>
> Young trans-kids need to know they were not born that way, and that most will no longer have a desire to change genders once they grow into adulthood. Parents need to know that up to 94 percent of school-age kids who identify as transgender will grow out of their desire to change genders as adults—if parents and schools stop encouraging them to internalize and publicize their LGBT identities.[10]

Dr. Joseph Berger is a Distinguished Life Fellow of the American Psychiatric Association and a Fellow of the Royal College of Physicians and Surgeons of Canada. His words speak to the dangers when schools embrace programs that support and, by their support, promote transgenderism in children:

> Transgendered people are people who claim that they are or wish to be people of the sex opposite to which they were born, or to which their chromosomal configuration attests. Sometimes, some of these people claim that they are "a woman trapped in a man's body" or alternatively "a man trapped in a woman's body." Scientifically, there is no such thing. The medical treatment of *delusions, psychosis or emotional happiness* is not by surgery.[11]

"ONE RIGHT WAY" INSTRUCTION:
MY . . . HOW TEACHING HAS CHANGED!

Lest there be misunderstanding, the oppositional views to the LGBTQI agenda presented here are not advanced to debunk the issue of transgenderism or to render judgment as to its validity and/or socially appropriateness. As a sexual construct, this condition remains a matter for scientific and, most certainly, public debate. The status of this condition is more of a question than it is a scientifically or culturally defined proposition. But there remain other unanswered questions as well, these having to do with the topic of teacher evaluation.

First is the question of why teachers have become so *onboard* in their support and *promotion* of a phenomenon that is so incompletely understood. A second question, the central matter in teacher evaluation practice today, is why principals have remained aloof from addressing the teachers in what they are doing. In the school district herein referenced, the teachers do not teach students *about* the issue of transgenderism, presenting the current state of the pros and cons of the phenomenon. They teach that the phenomenon is both scientifically valid and culturally appropriate. And their principals make no evaluative assessment of this one-sided pedagogy. The matter of "tolerance" is often raised should any discussion ensue.

It is well, and also good, that teachers teach their students tolerance. Historically, tolerance has been taken to mean that a person should allow for the beliefs and practices of another, even when these may be in conflict with his or her own. Allowing for differences, so long as they are not deemed detrimental, is a worthy social construct for a civilized society. However, tolerance has always been taken to mean that the rightness and well-being of intent and outcome are a part of the social equation of something to be tolerated.

In short, there have always been *standards* as to what constitutes what is right, proper, and appropriate, not detrimental to the greater good of the people. Not *every* act or behavior should be tolerated, as if all are right and nondetrimental. For example, no one tolerates burglary, murder, or thuggery! In short, the *truth* of a matter must enter as a tempering agent in order for tolerance to have a societally acceptable meaning.

But today the meaning of tolerance has changed, and particularly so in the public schools regarding how teachers choose to teach about it. In their book, *The New Tolerance*, Josh McDowell and Bob Hostetler define how the definition of "tolerance" has been changed:

> In contrast to traditional tolerance, which asserts that everyone has an equal right to believe or say what he thinks is right, the new tolerance —the way children are being taught to believe—says that what every individual believes or says is equally right, equally valid. So not only does everyone have an equal right to his beliefs, but all beliefs are equal. All values are equal. All truth claims are equal.[12]

The school district herein referenced provides an example of this *new tolerance* teaching approach. In this district the board of education–approved health curriculum purports to teach students about some socially sensitive issues. In so doing it engages outside speakers, people who come into the classrooms to talk to students about their areas of specialization. But are those speakers behaving as teachers or indoctrinators?

In this district, the outside speakers who come in to address LGBTQI issues are *all* from organizations that support or promote the LGBTQI agenda.[13] Ostensibly, these speakers are brought in to help any LGBTQI student feel comfortable and accepted, based on *student safety*. But in so doing, they focus their presentations on teaching students that the LGBTQI agenda is both legitimate and appropriate.

And because they present no other view of the topic, they become advocates for a cause, not educators. What's more problematic is that *no* speakers are solicited to come into classrooms to provide students a dissention point of view. Students get but one side of this story, the advocacy side. Students receive just the *one-way thinking* that conforms with the speaker's agenda!

Given what is presently known about the phenomenon of sexual identity issues, why are teachers not *evaluated* for their teaching what has not been established as academic truth? *Teaching* in a spirit of tolerance is a good thing, but *advocating* to students that LGBTQI matters are to be accepted at face value, absent questioning their legitimacy of veracity, becomes a matter of indoctrination. As such, it has no place in a public school classroom! This issue is *flying under the radar* at the school and also in the community. And it continues to "fly" largely because it remains unaddressed by school principals in their formal teacher evaluation procedures.

The only form of teacher evaluation brought to bear on this matter occurs if/when a teacher chooses not to support the district's policy guidelines. In the school district herein described, a teacher referencing a student as male, when that student chooses to "identify" as female, will get into serious trouble with the school district: "The intentional or persistent refusal to respect a student's gender identity (for example, intentionally referring to the student by a name or pronoun that does not correspond to the student's gender identity) is a violation of these Guidelines."[14] In other words, if a student named *Max* decides that he wants to be called *Maxine*, that becomes the reality teachers are *required* to abide. No exceptions will be tolerated!

Once again, addressing this subject in this school district is not seeking to render an adjudication of this condition, either positive or negative. While the presentation of the facts may seem excessively negative toward the sexual identity issue it addresses, the sole intent is to portray clearly that teachers are performing their duties inappropriately, and that they are not being held accountable for their performance by their principals. In short, these teachers are engaging in *education malpractice*, while not being held to account for their actions in any formal evaluative manner.

Some might think that what has been described in this district is an anomaly, something that is rare in occurrence and not found in most other school districts across the country. But be mindful that the district herein described is a large metropolitan one, one of approximately thirty thousand students. It resides in a city that hosts a major university, one with a long-established school of education. As such, it is considered by many to be a school district that surely *must* represent right and proper educational practices. Many boards of education look to this school district as a model for what they then decide is proper procedure in their own school districts.

Many school districts across the country, university town or not, are adopting similar rules and regulations. Like the school district herein described, these new policies address a worthy intent, providing for the safety and educational opportunities of their transgendered students. But in seeking to achieve it, the school district engages in overreach. While seeking to protect students from abuse because of a condition the students manifest, the school districts engage in sanctioning the condition itself, an unnecessary and inappropriate circumstance. The frontline agent for supporting this overreach is the school principal. But in so doing, the principal must forfeit a meaningful teacher evaluation paradigm. The question of *one-sided teaching* cannot be addressed if the district's policies are to be enforced.

However, over two thousand years of human history and common sense speak to an opposing view. These board-enacted policies, while providing for the necessary protection of students, do not make clear that no issues, including sexual identity issues, are to be presented in an *advocacy* format. As a result, some teachers, advocates themselves for the LGBT agenda, have seized the opportunity to use their classrooms to advance a cause. This is wrong, but it is not being addressed through any form of evaluation process that would sanction teachers, those choosing to behave in the capacity of special-interest advocates.

The result of this situation being allowed to continue is that educational advocacy supplants the sound practice of teaching. And with no one addressing this behavior in an *evaluative* manner, it continues unabated. Students are subjected to one point of view by their teachers, and parents are unaware that their children are being lobbied to favor one-way-thinking and not "thinking" itself. And while one might hope that this practice is not common, such is not the case. There are many more examples of administrators failing to evaluate their teachers for what they are teaching, and in different categories of unacceptable teaching practice.

A FOOTNOTE TO THE GENDER ISSUE: WHY ARE TEACHERS, AND THEIR PRINCIPALS, SO ACQUIESCENT?

Some of the teachers referenced in the matter described here are *active* participants in advocating for a position representing their own personal beliefs. Other teachers are also participating by way of their default position of silence. It would strain credulity to believe that the majority of the teachers in the school would hold the beliefs of the transgender-advocate teachers. So as unsettled and controversial as this issue is, why do the rest of the teachers merely go along with an issue about which they might have opposing views?

As referenced earlier, the board of education in this school district has codified what it *requires* to be done, and not done, by teachers in the district. If a male student, one whom his parents named "John" at birth, now decides that he is "Joan," the teachers are now *ordered*, by the board of education, to refer to him as "Joan." Unless teachers are willing to abide being subject to sanctions, those imposed by the school district, they have no choice.

Regardless of whether or not they believe in the sexual construct in question as a valid issue of self-identity, they are now ordered not only to *tolerate* this student's behavior, but to *participate* in it. Their *required* participation is evidenced by the fact that they are called upon to address the student as he or she wishes, but most certainly not by his or her birth name. Failing to do so will result in retribution from their supervisors!

One might wonder why they allow themselves to be so easily coerced by a board of education in such an important matter. Some teachers might say, "Well, I don't have any of them in my classroom, so why get into it?" But that's like waiting for the fire to start before going out to buy a fire extinguisher! And is this a proper posture for a teacher, one wishing to be identified as a "professional"?

This is an example of a *fraudulent* teacher evaluation paradigm, for both teachers and the principals who evaluate them. First, teachers allow themselves to be placed into the position of accepting an academically dishonest proposition. Second, the same teachers accept, as valid and proper, the district's regulation that they should be sanctioned for failure to behaviorally adhere to the academically dishonest proposition. These evaluation criteria seem to be at odds with any reasoned definition of "professionalism."

In keeping with academic honesty, it would seem that they should be evaluated, and positively so, for refusing to accept board of education policies that fly in the face of common sense. Additionally, and perhaps more importantly, the issue of transgenderism has yet to be shown to be a legitimate social construct, yet alone one that should be promoted by the public schools. With so much yet to be known about matters of sexual identity, much of which will likely reinforce two sexes constituting "normalcy," one might wonder why school officials seem in a rush to inculcate a redefinition. And why are so many cowed into complying with their views?

Why do principals, their bosses, and others in the professional educational community refuse to take a position other than that adopted by LGBT lobbyists? The NASSP (National Association of Secondary School Principals), in its policy statement on transgender students, goes so far as to sanction the participation of transgender students in any sport they choose to participate in, on the basis of how they "identify," i.e., the sex they *choose* to be. If a male student (born male) chooses to "identify" as a female, then he is free to play on the girls' basketball team.[15]

For decades teachers have been lobbying the public to recognize them as "professionals," in keeping with the respect afforded physicians and others of such status. But allowing themselves to be placed in such a nonprofessional "just following orders" role does not speak well for such a profession's ethical standards. The National Education Association, *the teachers' union*, also conforms to the politically correct agendas advanced by the LGBT lobby in its willful support of the LGBTQI agenda.[16]

Perhaps the only group of people who are coming forward to confront these issues is parents, the ones whose children are subjected to the widespread politically correct conformity promoted by these questionable "professionals": teachers, administrators, boards of education, and activist organizations. "In Portland, Oregon, parents of high school students have filed a federal lawsuit over the school district's policy that allows a biological female student who claims to be a male to use the boy's locker room and bathroom."[17] "Common sense? Not according to the parents!

Another classroom activity, this one unsanctioned by the school district, shows how noncurricular issues are being taught in public school classrooms, while escaping any form of evaluation. What's worse, were it not for a nationally broadcast television news program bringing it to air, this matter of educational malpractice would likely have gone completely unnoticed in the community wherein it took place. But even when brought to the attention of the community and the school "leadership," via a national airing of the district's "dirty laundry," nothing was done.

WHITE PEOPLE ARE PRIVILEGED PEOPLE: TEACHERS TEACHING "CRAP"

In the book *Super-Charged Learning*, the author describes a learning technique he titles "Making up Crap."[18] This learning strategy calls upon the student to associate the thing to be learned with something that is "crap"—something silly, nonsensical, absurd, having no foundation in reality. In so doing, the student locks in strong physical, visual, and emotional sensations to the thing he/she wants to learn. The thing to be learned is remembered easily because it has been infused with powerful *human* traits, those that serve to lock onto new information.

The point made is that we don't learn through the *words* that represent the thing to be learned, often dry and uninspiring, but through our *human traits*: our physical, visual, and emotional selves. In this learning heuristic, "crap" is a tool to be used to learn something, not the "something" to be learned! Not a vulgar term, "crap" simply refers to anything that is inherently goofy!

In one Wisconsin school, teachers seem to have become confused as to the appropriate role that "crap" is supposed to play in the classroom. Parents of middle-school students became aware that their children, twelve to fourteen years old, were given a "white privilege" test in their English classes.[19] The story made national headlines when it was reported in a segment of *Tucker Carlson Tonight*, the nationally televised show by Fox News, airing each evening at 8:00 p.m. EST.[20]

In a middle school in this district, a few English teachers gave their students a "white privilege" test that contained sixty-five items. The students were told to respond to each item by checking a box for each item with which they agreed. Here are some of the statements on the test:

- I have never been told that I "sound white."
- I never doubted my parents' acceptance of my sexuality.
- I feel comfortable in the gender I was born in.
- No one in my family has student loans.
- My family can afford a therapist.
- I feel privileged because of the identity I was born with.
- I am heterosexual.[21]

This "optional" test, *not* part of the approved curriculum in the district, was given to students in English language arts classes, ostensibly as a follow-up part of a class lesson dealing with civil rights.

One might assume that the sixty-five questions on this test would be relevant to the defined topic, civil rights, in the judgments of the teachers giving the test; more than just one teacher gave this test. But what possible linkage could there be in asking a student any of the questions just cited?! One might also wonder what all of this has to do with "English language arts" as well. But does this have anything to do with teacher evaluation?

In every public school district, boards of education are charged with approving *what* will be taught to the students in the district, resulting in an "approved district curriculum." This document contains the subject matter *allowed to be taught* to the students in the district. And while teachers are generally given latitude in utilizing class materials that are considered "ancillary" and/or "supportive" to this curriculum, these materials are not to be extraneous. They are not to be unrelated to the topics approved by their boards of education, those who are elected representatives of their community members. As such, board members serve to represent that which parents approve to be taught to their children.

Another function of boards of education is the hiring of teachers for their school districts. While school principals typically play a role in interviewing candidates for teaching positions in their schools, and superintendents recommend their choices to the board of education, it is the board members who approve these *professional* hires. In so doing, boards routinely require that teachers they hire sign a formal contract of employment in the school district. This document describes the behaviors that the teacher and the board agree will be engaged, by the teacher, during the term of the contract. The contract lists the standards to which teachers must adhere in order to teach in the district.

While *not* representing the standards for teachers in the school district wherein the "white privilege" survey was used, what follow are examples of standards that would be considered appropriate for inclusion in any teacher's contract. It would be difficult to believe that a school district or teacher would object to any of these:

The Teacher

- Uses instructional materials that are accurate and appropriate for the lesson being taught.
- Selects instructional materials and strategies based on their: relevance to students, foundational evidence base.
- Maintains respectful relationships with students, their families, and/or significant adults.
- Incorporates evidence-based strategies into lessons.
- Adheres to standards of professional practice.[22]

What should be clear is that the issuance of the "white privilege" tests by the teachers in this school constituted a breach of professional ethics. Two areas are of concern are (1) the teachers were teaching content that was out-of-bounds, not a part of the approved curriculum, and (2) the teachers were in violation of their *professional-status* responsibilities, as referenced above. They were in violation of their contractual obligations.

Given these circumstances, shouldn't the teachers' behaviors in this situation be included as a part of their formal performance evaluations? Shouldn't they, perhaps, even be reprimanded for their unprofessional actions? One would think so. But in this instance, one would be wrong!

GAME-SET-MATCH!
A TEACHER EVALUATION OPPORTUNITY . . . A TEACHER EVALUATION FAILURE

In his writing, Ernest Hemingway focused assiduously on telling the truth. Hemingway indicated that any writer wanting to become proficient at his/her craft needed to be able to discern fact from fiction: "The most essential gift for a good writer is a built-in, shockproof, [expletive] detector."[23] Discerning the difference between "expletive" and truth, in Hemingway's view, was essential for truth-telling in what one might write about any subject.

In a classroom in the school scenario described, it was one student, "immature" by commonly accepted standards of development, who possessed the insight to see that the teacher was dispensing questionable information. While reports do not identify this student as a boy or girl, this student knew intuitively that what the teacher was teaching was wrong! The parent who received this report from this student also knew that what was going on in that classroom was out-of-bounds. The question of why both an immature adolescent and a parent would see this, but that a teacher with "professional" standing could not, defies a credible answer.

What this scenario brings to mind is that *some* teachers today have increasingly taken to introducing their own political/ideological agendas into their classroom teaching, be they subtle or overt. As this practice is clearly in violation of their professional status and responsibilities, it *should* be addressed via the formal evaluation processes that are the province of the building principal. Such behavior as was exhibited in this "white privilege" test issue should have been stopped, and the teacher/s in question censured formally for the behavior they engaged. But is this what happened in this case? Sadly, the answer is "No!"

In the aftermath of the "white privilege" test scenario in this school, the principal indicated that he will *not* be addressing their behaviors in their formal evaluations. He indicated that the teachers involved, apparently three in number, are some of his best teachers.[24] And while this kind of situation might seem unusual, it is not. What this building principal decided *not* to do is not at all out of character with his colleagues across the country. This, and other widespread incidences of failures to properly evaluate teaching performance, is becoming increasingly more common in the nation's public schools.

THE EXPANSIVENESS OF INADEQUATE TEACHER EVALUATION:
WHAT LIES BEYOND THE SUBJECT MATTER

The two examples of inappropriate schooling given here, examples that deal with things that are not subject-specific (i.e., they're not about science, mathematics, etc.), show that teacher evaluation has *many* aspects. Its application extends beyond just subject-matter content and presentation. But what is evident in these two cases is that the task of teacher evaluation is not being accomplished properly, and sometimes is not accomplished at all. A new report on public education suggests why this state of affairs exists today:

> *The Widget Effect* is a wide-ranging report that studies teacher eval-uation and dismissal in four states and 12 diverse districts and re-flects survey responses from approximately 15,000 teachers and 1,300 administrators.
>
> Effective teachers are the key to student success, yet our school systems treat all teachers as interchangeable parts, not professionals. Excellence goes unrecognized and *poor performance goes unad-dressed.* This indifference to performance disrespects teachers and gambles with student lives.[25] (emphasis mine)

What happened in the school in Wisconsin is not unusual. It is but another example of a situation wherein a teacher's behaviors in the classroom, *wrong* behaviors, are ignored by their supervisors. Like many such incidents, this one *flew under the radar* of a public school district. It went unnoticed in the district because it went unaddressed at the school. An issue of inappropriate teaching behavior was neither identified nor appropriately addressed by school officials before parents became involved in protesting the behavior.

Many such issues are not being addressed in the public schools today. They are not coming to light for a variety of reasons, of which far-reaching *political correctness* in the public schools looms very large. Myriad problems within the school administration, both in structure and function, account for much of what results in poor teacher evalua-tion systems today.

These failures in teacher evaluation systems are not just present in the school districts described in the scenarios here. They are pervasive across virtually every school district, large and small, in the country. And as powerful as these examples of miseducation and education mal-practice are, an even more important teacher evaluation issue exists in public education today. While teachers are teaching what they are *not* supposed to be teaching, and not being properly evaluated for doing so, they are simultaneously not being properly evaluated for what they are *supposed* to be teaching. Both of these are taking place in public schools throughout the country today, and they have yet to be effective-ly addressed by the people who are in positions to do so.

To begin to do so, three questions must be addressed in public-school education today: Who is responsible for evaluating teachers, what is being evaluated, and how is it being done? This is discussed in chapter 3.

3

THE WAY WE ARE

The Current State of Teacher Evaluation

Effective teaching is dependent upon the interactivity of two factors, each of which is additive but not solely determinative. These coalesce to result in a teaching performance outcome. And it *is* a *performance*. Much as a performer in the "performing arts" (theater, film, music, etc.) seeks to *engage* an audience via a performance, so too does a teacher seek to engage with students via a performance. However, the outcomes sought in each of these venues dictate much different kinds of performances.

A performer in the arts seeks to engage the visual, physical, and emotional mental states of an audience to result in an entertaining and enjoyable experience—a successful performance. The audience may inadvertently experience *learning* through watching the performance, but learning is not the goal in the performing arts; entertainment is the goal. In teaching, the same human characteristics of the visual, physical, and emotional are involved. But in teaching, the goal is not entertainment. It is *learning*.

In public schools today, the principal is *the* person charged with the responsibility to assure that quality teaching is taking place. This is the person responsible for evaluating the performances of the teachers. The prevailing thinking is that a good teaching performance results in learning, whereas a poor teaching performance results in a lesser amount, or no learning. It is the principal's job to determine the good teaching from the poor teaching, and all variations in between.

Assuming the position of a teacher evaluation expert, the principal ostensibly possesses the knowledge and skills necessary for assessing the quality of a teaching performance. As a *teacher of teachers*, the principal views, assesses, and critiques a teacher's performance, afterward proffering suggestions for improvement. The quality of the teaching taking place in classrooms is the sole responsibility of the school principal. But are principals *qualified* to carry out this responsibility?

THE FRAUD OF TEACHER EVALUATION: SETTING THE TABLE

As previously stated, "fraud" is an act that serves to deceive or mislead people. An act of fraud presents something as something that it is not. As an act of deception, fraud may have many faces. It can be an act of purpose, conspiratorially planned and carried out by one or more persons to deceive others. Or it may be inadvertent, occurring more by an accident of circumstance than a purposed design. The fraud of teacher evaluation is likely of the second kind, although the behaviors of some of those associated with it arouse suspicion that they may be acting in willful complicity. More about that later.

In teacher evaluation fraud, the process of teacher evaluation is presented as something it is not. It is presented as a process whereby the quality of teaching can be determined *adequately*; poor, good, excellent, etc. Through actions taken by school principals, an accurate assessment of a teacher's effectiveness can be ascertained. But is this true? The answer is "no," and the truth of this answer is animated by the word "adequately." The on-the-ground reality is that teacher evaluation, as it is currently constituted in today's public schools, cannot and does not properly evaluate a teacher's performance in the classroom.

As will be seen, many comingling entities align to generate this result. These are no way coconspirators, but merely members of what could be called an *education coterie*. This group, the coterie, is made up of people and organizations associated with public education. Coterie *members* act in virtual lockstep in the positions they support, in issues involving the public schools. A bureaucracy of bureaucracies, the coterie is a made up of special-interest groups, all of which seek to maintain their influence in what takes place in the public schools.

The National Education Association, American Federation of Teachers, Association for Supervision and Curriculum Development, National Association for Secondary School Principals (NASSP), National Association of Elementary School Principals, (NAESP), National School Boards Association, and the National Parent Teacher Association are some of the groups composing this loosely knit agglomeration of special interests.

Coterie members have traditionally centered their activities on the interests of their respective memberships, such as the NASSP advocating for secondary school principal issues. However, in recent years coterie interests have expanded into areas well beyond these. Largely energized by the forces of political correctness, coterie members have seemingly joined forces with what have become known as "social justice" advocacy groups. Several coterie agents now engage in the active insinuation of these issues into the public schools.

Historically, the appropriate role of public education has been to teach students *how* to think, not *what* to think. And while fact-based data such as historical dates and scientific principles have been routinely taught as "what" issues, they have been taught in an agenda-neutral context. But as was seen earlier, this has changed in recent years. With schools now engaging activists to teach their special-interest agendas, the political agendas and positions of some have now found their routing into the public schools, thereby teaching students *what* to think.

Coterie member groups are increasingly choosing to engage with these politically correct, "social justice" issues, the business of special-interest groups. As these are largely unrelated to the *appropriate* role of public education, that of teaching how to think and not what to think, coterie memberships are now engaging in political activism under the guise of supporting education. This is wholly inappropriate. While more about workings of the coterie will come later, suffice it to say that it exerts a *powerful* influence on everything happening in the public schools today. And so far, they have gone unchallenged!

The school principal is the on-the-ground agent conducting teacher evaluations in the schools. This person is *100 percent* responsible for teacher evaluation. As such, the principal is the focus of why teacher evaluation does not accomplish what it purports to accomplish . . . why it is fraudulent. But as these men and/or women engage in this process, keep in mind that nowhere in the pages to come is it suggested that they are singularly culpable for this fraud, acting entirely alone.

As will be shown, principals find themselves in a situation of neither their desire nor their making. The principal's *situation* is acted upon by others, those involved in not only influencing principals' behaviors, but in demanding them to be in accord with the wishes of the others. These *others* are the heretofore referenced education coterie memberships. While principals are singularly responsible for the evaluation of teachers, many others, acting together in near unison, promote the realization of an outcome they desire. They will be described, and their influence detailed, later.

Principals find themselves in the untenable position of denying the presence of the *elephant in the room*. In the matter of teacher evaluation, this pachyderm represents a failed system that has never been addressed for what it is, and what it cannot be, in the past and in the current day. But however principals came to be in this situation, the teacher evaluation process is defined by what they are unable to do. And as will be shown, while charged with the responsibility, they are unable to perform the task of teacher evaluation.

THE SCHOOL PRINCIPAL AS "INSTRUCTIONAL LEADER": A DARWINIAN EVENT GONE AWRY?

As was described in chapter 1, the evolution of teacher evaluation in the public schools was animated by circumstantial exigency. The position of school principal was originated as schools grew larger. As pupil populations grew, there arose a need for a person to perform various administrative tasks, such as ordering textbooks and supplies, scheduling classes, etc. When the position was created in the mid-1800s, the principal's job was limited to these kinds of routine tasks.

The role of educational leadership to include instructional assessments, evaluating one's colleagues' teaching, was not part of the original game plan. As was stated earlier, principals were never thought to be the school's *intellectual* leaders. They were school managers. They functioned in areas of school governance and control that related to the students, those only peripherally affecting teachers and their teaching activities. Teachers retained the high degree of autonomy in their class-room teaching activities that was always theirs to determine.

As school and teacher populations grew, the governing bodies charged with overseeing them began to see a need for the supervision and evaluation of the workforce, the teachers. To address this need, principals were asked to expand their largely managerial roles to include the oversight of teachers and their teaching activities. While they continued to dedicate the majority of their time to their managerial duties, principals now began to enter classrooms to watch teachers as they taught their classes.

Today, principals find themselves defined as "instructional leaders," and less so as agents of governance or management. This *role flip* in job responsibility occurred incrementally over time and almost without notice to the present day. Today, instructional leadership is seen as the correct and proper number-one job for principals. But do the day-to-day activities of principals comport well with their new role redefinition? Does this relatively recent change in job responsibilities reflect what principals actually *do*, or is it more of an assertion of what they *should* be doing?

In a presentation at the University of California in April of 2017, Harvard University president Dr. Lawrence Bacow made a statement about leadership that, unfortunately, may portray the daily activities of many school principals: "Leadership necessarily involves managing change. If you're not managing change, you're not leading . . . but presiding."[1] The role of *presiding* is one in which too many school principals find themselves today, not necessarily by choice, but by what was previously referenced as an evolutionary circumstance. This is existentially problematic because the principal's *leadership* role is viewed as one of high priority:

> Today, improving school leadership ranks high on the list of priorities for school reform. In a detailed 2010 survey, school and district administrators, policymakers, and others declared principal leadership among the most pressing matters on a list of issues in public school education. Teacher quality stood above everything else, but principal leadership came next, outstripping matters including dropout rates, STEM (science, technology, engineering, and math) education, student testing, and preparation for college and careers.[2]

"Principal leadership" and "teacher quality" are strongly interdependent in that they are, as seen in the previous statement, *the* two most important entities typically associated with programs of school reform. While principals have many responsibilities as the chief executive of the school, the highest ranking responsibility among these is *instructional* leadership. As is most typical, the principal expresses instructional leadership through a formally established teacher evaluation process.

Principals observe teachers in their classrooms and subsequently confer with them about what they saw in their observations. Principals provide an assessment of the positive and negative aspects, a critique of what was observed in the classroom during their visitations. Suggestions for improvements are then offered, those that teachers are expected to incorporate in their teaching.

The operational premise for this approach is that, through this interactive teacher evaluation process, teachers will improve their classroom teaching performances. Generated by the instructional leadership of the principal, this teacher evaluation process continues throughout the school year, ostensibly resulting in an overall improvement in instruction. This has been the lingua franca of teacher evaluation for decades. Teachers teach, principals sit and watch teachers teach, principals tell teachers what they think of what they saw, and teachers become better teachers as a result.

But does the principal's evaluation engagement with teachers actually accomplish the result of instructional improvement, that being better teaching? And if instructional improvement is *the* highest priority of principals, how much time during the school day do they dedicate to teacher evaluation activities, those that would result in instructional improvement? The answers to these questions do not seem to support the program's desired outcome of instructional improvement.

What does it mean for an administrator to be *an instructional leader*? As often as this phrase is repeated, you'd think there would be well-researched techniques with proven effectiveness. But there is less research on the topic than you'd think, and much of it (May, Huff, & Goldring, 2012) actually shows a weak or non-existent relationship between student achievement and the priority administrators place on instructional leadership (as opposed to other aspects of a principal's job, e.g., close attention to administrative matters, inspirational leadership, focus on school culture, etc.)

A new study by Jason Grissom, Susanna Loeb, and Ben Master shed light on the role of instructional leadership. The result showed that principals spent, on average, 12.6 percent of their time on activities related to instruction.[3]

A study at Stanford University reports:

> principals spent most of their time in the school office—54 percent of the day in their own offices and another nine percent elsewhere in the main school office. About 40 percent of principals' time was spent away from the school office in locations around campus including hallways, playgrounds, and classrooms. On average, the principals spent only about eight percent of the school day in classrooms.[4]

The most common view, both within the educational establishment and on the street, suggests that the school principal is the *leader* of the school. If this view is accurate, the principal is *the* person responsible for the quality of teaching in the school. It is the principal's responsibility to see to it that the quality of teaching is high. But as has been seen from the brief review of history detailed earlier, principals came to their instructional leadership roles largely by default, not by design.

Notwithstanding pronouncements by the present-day establishment that the main job of the school principal is instructional leadership, principals persevere in spending the majority of their time being managers, much as they did when the job of principal was created. As they were in earlier days, they find themselves miscast in a role they cannot play. But there's more.

As an unfortunate consequence of their *instructional leadership* ineptitude, principals' abilities to exert leadership in other areas within their school communities can be cast into doubt by teachers and others. More so than others not as closely associated with what takes place in schools, teachers know that their principals are absent the *subject-matter* skills, those necessary to assess their teaching abilities. Also, it is likely that some suspect that their principals might not have been very good teachers themselves when they were classroom teachers. But it probably doesn't end there.

The recognition that their supervisors are not able to exert leadership in their *first-order responsibility*, the improvement of instruction, creates space for another mindset to creep in. Perhaps their principals are incapable of leadership in other areas as well. Do they possess the ability to exert knowledge-based leadership in matters of student discipline, curricular matters, or other school-related matters? While not voiced, some teachers may conclude, "Well, if they can't even do their most important job properly, why should I think they can do others very well?!"

PRINCIPALS = LEADERSHIP?
A CURRENT-DAY ABDICATION EXAMPLE

As was described in chapter 2, schools have become veritable petri dishes for social-project experimentation, some of which many teachers and community members likely would oppose, were they asked. And this has been accomplished absent any pushback by the ostensible leadership in the schools—the principals. Is it likely that the majority of teachers are in agreement with this? Or do some, perhaps many, wonder why no one has seen fit to object? And whom can they look to for leadership, those to whom they might voice their objections? Would those not be the same people who have remained so silent, their principals?

A recently published book, *When Harry Became Sally*,[5] addresses a hot-topic subject of the day, transgenderism. As was discussed in chapter 2, this topic has become prominent in many schools across the country, calling upon school leaders to address it.

> A teacher at Rocklin Academy Family of Schools (RAFOS) read "I am Jazz," a story about an 11-year-old transgender student, aloud to a kindergarten class in June 2017. That same month, RAFOS Principal Jillayne Antoon presented a five-year-old boy to the child's class at a "transgender reveal party" and identified him by a new name and sex, saying the boy had become a girl. Parents were not given advance notice of either event.[6]

Unlike this principal, most public school principals have remained relatively noncommittal. In these socially volatile issues, those that have the potential to change the curriculum and culture of their schools, principals have found little middle ground in which they might act. Not wishing to be found personally accountable for taking what would be perceived as a false step, many resort to higher authorities, their super-intendent bosses. But as principals defer in such matters, are their teachers concluding that they might not have the wherewithal to lead in *any* venue?

And what about parents in the community, those whose children are subject to the curriculum and culture of the schools they attend? Might they too wonder at their school principal's silence? Might not the parents of a high school girl, a student-athlete wrestler, take exception to a male student-athlete wrestler competing against their daughter?! While this specific situation will be discussed in the next section, suffice it to say that such a situation presents a very clear student-safety issue, one that the school principal should most certainly address.

While the capacity to lead in other areas remains in question, such as the safety of student-athletes, the discussion here remains that of whether or not principals are competent to evaluate their teachers. While well suited for many of the responsibilities listed in their job descriptions, school principals are not qualified for the role of instructional leadership. The discussion to come, reviewing the various factors influencing their status as school principals, will show why they are not. One set of circumstances that constrains principals from being *real* leaders in their schools, not merely presiders over circumstances, is next.

SCHOOL PRINCIPALS:
WHO ARE THEY, WHAT THEY DO, HOW THEY DO IT

A mother knocks on her son's bedroom door in the morning to awaken him for school. In a loud voice she announces, "Tom, get out of bed now or you'll be late for school!" From behind the closed door comes the whimpering response, "No! I don't *want* to go! Please don't make me go! The kids make fun of me and all the teachers pick on me!" Undeterred, his mother persists: "Now listen to me, Tom . . . you *have* to go! As we've discussed before, there are two very good reasons! First, you're 35 years old, and second . . . you're the principal!"

Schools can be a tough place for other than just the kids! And while most principals are not made fun of by the students or picked on by all the teachers, the jobs they do are so multifaceted that they may feel that way on some days. But principals have a very good idea of what they're getting into before they step into their offices for their first day of work. The reason for this is that principals were all teachers before they became principals.

WHERE DO PRINCIPALS COME FROM? SOURCING, BUT NOT OUTSOURCING

In the United States, public school principals are drawn from *one* field of work. They are all former teachers. As has been true since the positon of "principal" was created in the late 1800s, public school districts uniformly seek their school principals from their teaching ranks. Only a handful of states currently hire superintendents of schools from noneducation backgrounds, having been neither teachers nor principals. While more states are exploring this format, all still require principals to have teaching experience.[7] But this practice is changing elsewhere.

England, experiencing a teacher shortage, now engages nonteaching candidates for the positon of "head," the functional equivalent of "principal" in the United States. England abandoned its requirement that head teachers possess Qualified Teacher Status in 2001.[8] The thought behind this change is that the *head* of a school does not need to possess expertise in every aspect of the school, so long as a team of people with varied competencies surround the head, compensating for any areas wherein the head is not competent.

But in the United States, the education coterie, largely influenced by university colleges of education, has been resistant to this change. While candidates with no teaching backgrounds are slowly gaining acceptance by the education coterie for superintendent positions, principals are still required to have been teachers before becoming eligible to become principals. Resistance to changing this institutionalized norm has some roots in university colleges of education, wherein professors of education wish to retain their status as the sole educators-of-educators, thus retaining their positions as players in the principal-hiring pipeline.

For decades these professors of education have retained a monopoly on the question of *who* may become a school-level leader, a principal. Through restrictive course requirements, and recently through protracted "internships" for prospective principals, they have retained firm control of who can become a principal. If this were to change so that, for example, a successful business entrepreneur could qualify to be hired as a principal, their training function would lose a substantial amount of its relevance. Not a good thing for a full-employment economy for professors of education!

What's wrong with the current situation whereby only teachers can be hired as principals, is that university colleges of education have failed to recognize that leadership in the public schools *can* be informed from outside its own ranks. The example of the varied skill sets applying over a broad range of workplace venues is commonplace in the world of business. One example comes from an unlikely source: the *bun* business!

Kat Cole, a former Hooters Girl, became the president of Cinnabon. Clearly, her workplace experiences at Hooters did not "qualify" her for the bun business. But they did not keep her from transferring what she knew about one kind of work, one she *knew*, to another kind of work, one she *didn't* know. She, and fortunately also Cinnabon, knew that hiring a person with wide-ranging skill sets was smarter than hiring a person with narrowly tailored skills, applicable to but one work venue. Cole's skills had broad *transfer quality*.

While her skill sets as a Hooters Girl didn't closely comport with a largely different business model, she had qualities that did. Of these she says:

> I can see the possible in people and situations where other people can't. And because I can see it, I can help other people see it. The domino effect of every human interaction, it goes somewhere. And so if you can be a part of seeing what's possible and helping other people see what's possible or just helping them lean in a more positive than negative in any given moment, the trajectory that you put the whole world on, is pretty phenomenal. [9]

University colleges of education and the professors inhabiting them, education coterie members, tend to promote a closed system of selecting school principals, one that manifests a kind of intellectual arrogance. The view that only formally trained teachers are qualified to be school principals presupposes that these teachers are superior to those absent this training. Another coterie assumption seems to assert that teachers, defined to be the only ones qualified to become principals, are uniquely different from all other groups of working people—farmers, assembly-line workers, medical doctors, lawyers, etc.

As the group-think goes, teachers are somehow uniquely qualified to be leaders of their own kind because they alone possess qualifications that are unavailable to those in business, industry, or any other profession. Unlike other workplace situations, why would teachers countenance only a person who has been *one of them* to supervise them? "No outsider need apply" seems to be the mindset in principal-training programs. Colleges and universities reinforce this mindset through their very special curricula for principal training and certification, available *only* to teachers.

WHO CAN BECOME A PRINCIPAL?
MANY ARE CALLED . . . AND MANY ARE CHOSEN

University colleges of education allow only teachers to enter their principal-training programs, master's degree programs for school administration. But beyond this initial gate-keeping restriction, they admit almost *every* teacher who makes application to their programs. The master's degree programs offered by colleges of education, offering certification programs in educational administration, admit nearly all teachers who make application for entry. With a valid teaching degree and some teaching experience, and one or two generic letters of recommendation, entrance to these graduate programs is, with rare exception, a sure-thing guarantee.

While teaching experience is required, there is little information required for admission to principal-training programs that would assess the quality of the *teaching* performances candidates bring to these programs. Letters of recommendation for these programs are commonly written by the teachers' immediate supervisors, their principals. But school principals are restricted by law from offering much other than generic information, nothing very critical. And so what colleges of education receive from them is of little value in determining who is a good candidate, and who might not be. These letters are mostly filled with little valuable information, particularly as they might relate to a candidate's ability to evaluate quality teaching in others.

On-the-ground classroom performance evaluation information is not information they can provide a college of education, one considering a teacher for its principal-training program. Accruing to legal constraints that pertain to releasing a district's human resources files, principals' recommendations avoid any references to a teacher's specific teaching deficiencies. Therefore, colleges of education cannot make well-informed determinations regarding the teaching proficiencies of those they admit to their principal-training programs.

What results from these relatively loosely structured entrance criteria is a system that admits virtually every applicant, absent an ability to control for the quality of its applicants' *teaching* ability. In short, being an excellent teacher is not a factor in gaining acceptance to these programs, because information of that nature cannot be ascertained by selection committees. A teacher's teaching ability does not inform the selection process for gaining admittance to a principal-training program.

If the number-one job of a principal is the assessment of quality teaching, it would seem that those selected to be principals should themselves be high-quality teachers. They should be the *only* ones considered for becoming principals. Additionally, it would be reasonable to expect that these excellent teachers should also have the ability, or at least the potential ability, to transmit that which they know to others. There should be some form of assessment of these characteristics. But as is demonstrated by college of education graduate degree requirements, those leading to licensing of principals, this is not the case.

PRINCIPAL TRAINING: THE UNIVERSITY COLLEGE OF EDUCATION

To become a principal, one must complete a formal program of coursework prescribed by professors in colleges of education. These professors, most of whom are from the ranks of former teachers and/or administrators, teach aspiring principals what is defined as a unique form of leadership: "education" leadership. The premise of "education" leadership professors seems to be that the principles of leadership in education are somehow unique to education, different from those in other work venues. But is this true?

While many university courses are required for the completion of a master's degree program and the fulfillment of principal certification criteria, most courses are not education-specific at all. While referring to "school" leadership, it is clear that no such specificity to course content is evident, at least as in *course descriptions*. A "required" course, this from a large teacher-training institution, shows how non-unique these principal-training courses are:

EAD 806: The Evolving Practice of School Leaders
As the first in a two-course sequence (EAD 806 and EAD 807), this course provides the foundation for continued study in the masters in educational administration program. A core belief of this program—and of this course—is that school leadership must prioritize quality instruction for all students as its main mission. Grounded in this belief, students explore the work of school-level leaders.

Two primary questions will guide learning: 1) what does it mean to be a leader? and 2) what does it mean to lead others? In the process of exploring these two questions, students are introduced to a core body of leadership knowledge including the history of school leadership, enduring leadership problems, leadership ethics, and promising leadership practices and theories. Students are asked to *acquire new knowledge*, challenge existing assumptions, and step outside of existing comfort zones.

Other key components of this course include the development of critical reading, writing, and reflection skills; communication skills; and a philosophy of ethical leadership. Students can also expect to cultivate rich collegial relationships with your classmates, learn more about themselves as leaders, and to conceptualize individual roles in school improvement.[10] (emphasis mine)

One might wonder how "acquire new knowledge," combined with other largely generic criteria, make this class uniquely applicable to *educational* leadership.

Another university teacher-training program lists courses for prospective school principals, each similarly displaying no unique *education* application:

ED 601 Leadership through Inquiry
ED 603 Shaping Organizations
ED 604 Understanding People

ED 605 External Environments
ED 665 Policy Analysis and Development[11]

As is the case with many other such "required courses" for the attainment of a degree in educational administration, the course material at this institution is generic in terms of what it teaches about leadership. Some other examples of course offerings from this institution, also specific to training principals, are Leadership and Organizational Development, Shared Leadership in Schools, and Education Finance and Policy.[12]

But except for the inclusion of an *education* reference in their titles, these courses do not appear to teach management/leadership skills that are unique to education. They are areas commonly found in management training programs for many different fields of work. These citations, and others, would not be recognizable as uniquely applicable for training to become a leader in an education venue were the reference to *education* not included in the course description.

And while some skill sets may be unique to *school* leadership, these can be learned equally well by people from outside the K-12 school establishment, as well as by those from within it. As was shown by former Hooters Girl Kat Cole, most of the qualities that make a person a good leader are found across a broad spectrum of work experience venues. They are universal in where and how they can be applied elsewhere.

While these course offerings are questionable regarding their education-specific nature, other courses that are included in principal-training programs reveal that they too are not education-specific, but they are *very* specific in another regard! They are specific to what has become a highly politicized *social justice* agenda in major universities across the country. The social justice agenda seeks to conform the thinking of university attendees to a strictly enforced code of political correctness, something heretofore thought to be anathema in a university environment. Once again, the *what to think*, in place of *how to think*, becomes evident in institutions of higher learning purporting to train those for higher positions in public education.

These politically correct course *requirements* breed a group-think in prospective school principals, one that will enhance their acceptance of soon-to-come demands made by the agenda-driven organizations in their communities. In virtually all these courses, the concept of unquestioned acceptance of virtually any and all forms of "diversity" are to be accepted and promoted in the public schools. "Diversity is good" is the mantra promulgated by colleges of education across the country today!

An example of this focus was seen in the LGBT circumstance cited in chapter 2. There, radical special-interest groups were shown to have made substantial inroads into the public schools. They had been successful in promoting and advancing their beliefs by engaging the *active participation* of the schools. Legitimizing their agenda, by *destigmatizing* the aberrant behaviors their adherents engage, is their strategy for achieving a dramatic change in societal norms. This is their endgame: normalizing the abnormal.

And beyond the community schools, their efforts have extended into principal-training programs at the university level. A course at a large teacher-training institution in the same community speaks to the success of their efforts: Slashing Stigmas: Promoting Positive Behaviors is one of several required classes at that university.[13] But is the matter of "slashing stigmas" a good thing, in all cases? Are there not *some* behaviors believed to be socially unacceptable in the culture today, those being quite worthy of stigmatization? And who gets to decide? Apparently, from this university's course description, university professors do!

Many undergraduate university programs have jumped onboard with the LGBT agenda as is evidenced by their course offerings (Lesbian and Gay Studies, Queer Identities in Contemporary Cultures, Intersections of Race, Class, Gender, and Sexuality).[14] As a result, universities' principal-training programs have engaged a form of radical mission creep by embracing these kinds of radical social issues in their graduate programs. As stated, the university professors know what's the right "what" to think about many issues, and they teach this *right thinking* to their students.

Whether or not these kinds of courses have a proper place in teacher and principal training is not considered a *politically correct* question for the asking, and so they continue to proliferate in colleges of education across the country. And what teacher, seeking principal licensure, is going to question this politically driven group-think?! In the environment that commonly extols the virtue of the bizarre in place of common sense, who will risk the censure of professors, and likely even classmates, by venturing a dissenting view? The answer: few if any!

But a dissenting view has relevance, or should have relevance. What do these kinds of subjects have to do with *leadership*, and what do they have to do with a principal's ability to assess teaching ability? Furthermore, how is it deemed appropriate that a university, supposedly the center of thoughtful inquiry and dissent, becomes the place where conforming views to only one set of beliefs is promoted? It would seem that teaching *what* to think in place of *how* to think would constitute educational malpractice. More about this later.

And while these *fringe* classes have become insinuated into the principal-training curriculum, classes that focus on teacher evaluation and what constitutes good teaching are largely absent. As any catalog of graduate studies for a master's degree in school administration will show, a great deal of the coursework required is of the kind that is either nonspecific to schooling or is only peripherally related to the education venue. What is taught and how it is taught, subject content and pedagogy, are not center stage in university colleges of education. These have become diluted, reduced in importance, vis-à-vis a plethora of activist-agenda coursework now a part of principal-training programs. And as stated, many of these courses now highlight "diversity" as their central theme.

INEPTITUDE:
THE PRINCIPAL'S "CATCH-22"

The two main components of quality teaching, subject-matter competence and pedagogical skills, receive little attention in principal-training programs. There are few, if any, courses offered that would help principals become better able to evaluate the teaching performances of their teachers, those teaching across a wide span of subject areas: biology, chemistry, Spanish, English, algebra, calculus, history, etc. Perhaps the reason no such courses are offered is due to the fact that no class would be able to bring about this result!

But having strong subject-matter competence, *knowing your stuff*, is but half of what makes for a good teacher. Teachers also need to be able to effectively *transmit* what they know to their students. A teacher needs to have a so-called bag of tricks, a repertoire of teaching techniques that can help to get the point across. These are the teacher's *pedagogical* skills. These teachers have the ability to, as the saying goes, *put the hay down where the goats can get it!*

Two empirically obvious facts continue to escape notice of the education coterie, and particularly of university principal-training professors: (1) Principals are not *able* to evaluate their teachers' *subject-matter* competence. As a result, they cannot know whether or not their teachers are teaching accurate and true information to their students and (2) Because they may not have been excellent teachers themselves (principal-training programs do not select candidates based upon their teaching skills), principals are not qualified to assess the pedagogical expertise of their teachers. They may not *know* what constitutes the practice of competent teaching.

These two issues remain the Achilles' heel of teacher evaluation in the public schools today, the principal's "Catch-22." School principals are placed in the unenviable position of being asked to do a job that they cannot do. In a word, principals are *inept* to do what they are being asked to do. They simply do not have the abilities to perform their teacher evaluation functions. And while absent the skills they need, *some* of these skills are outside the reach of principals—they simply cannot be ascertained. What a dilemma to know that you don't have the skills to do your job, and you can't get them!

When a principal enters a classroom to evaluate a teacher, these are the two areas of teacher performance (subject competence and pedagogical expertise) that principals must address. In order to render an effective and accurate assessment of the quality of the teaching performance observed, the principal must possess competence in both. If inept in either, the validity of the evaluation is subject to serious question. So what's the current state of principals' ability in each, and why is it that way?

THE SCHOOL PRINCIPAL: A COMMAND OF CONTENT?

As previously stated, all principals come to their positions through the experience of having been classroom teachers. For example, a high school principal may have been a biology teacher previous to undergoing the graduate degree training to become a principal. As such, this principal is skilled in only one discipline: biology. This principal may have had a minor degree in undergraduate training, perhaps minoring in chemistry, but the major-degree coursework was in biology. As such, this principal *may* be qualified to evaluate those teachers teaching biology, and to a lesser degree, those teaching chemistry.

But herein resides a fallacy. This fallacy is that this principal possesses the requisite expertise to evaluate *either* biology or chemistry—both areas of undergraduate study. The principal is inept in this process because these two fields of science have changed over time, time since the principal left undergraduate school. Absent *active* engagement in these fields, it is unlikely that the principal will have kept up with the latest developments in each. While the university coursework the principal engaged in while a student may be adequate at the beginning of a teaching career, its content accuracy diminishes over time.

As examples, in biology, the number of orders of insects has changed in the past several years. In 1960, there were 26 orders of insects. Today there are either 29 or 32, depending on how entomologists classify them.[15] Also changing is the periodic table of the elements, which is applied in the study of chemistry. This table lists all the elements that exist in the natural world, both naturally occurring and man-made. Today, 118 elements are listed in this table. This number includes four man-made elements that were added in 2017—new elements.[16] The increasing prominence of quantum mechanics in schools' science curricula provides yet another example wherein subject-matter content is changing continuously.

But principals do not evaluate *just* classes in which they may have content-knowledge familiarity. For example, secondary school principals, middle school and high school, evaluate teachers across a curriculum containing *dozens* of subject-matter classes. Teachers are assigned class schedules deriving from their university degree-status expertise, typically teaching *only* subjects for which they are qualified to teach. But principals, having no qualification to teach but perhaps a few of these, evaluate how teachers teach *all* of them.

Principals find themselves observing teachers who are teaching subjects well outside their fields of knowledge—things about which they know nothing! How then can a principal give an accurate accounting of whether or not good teaching is taking place regarding the teaching of *true and accurate content*? As in the automobile brake-job example cited earlier, a supervisor evaluating something about which he/she has no knowledge cannot be expected to deliver a very good outcome.

And while these examples represent a secondary school context wherein specific *subjects* are taught, the content-knowledge problem evident therein impacts elementary school classrooms as well. There too, while in a more limited scope, teachers introduce students to specific subject matter: reading, writing, mathematics, and others. Each of these subject areas requires expertise, much of which may not be resident in the principal's knowledge base. Also, an elementary school curriculum focuses on showing children *how to learn*, as well as *what to learn*, a dramatically different learning circumstance than secondary teaching displays.

While the elementary classroom teacher spends considerable time explaining and showing their students *how to learn*, secondary teachers are largely focused on presenting information to be learned, spending little or no time showing students *how* to learn. Unlike elementary grade teachers, secondary teachers are closely associated with the professors at colleges and universities, where content takes precedence over process. They are largely dispensers of information.

Some people would say that principals "know enough" to evaluate their teachers. They have "an idea" of what's being taught, and this is enough to render judgments as to whether or not teachers are teaching true and accurate content. But if this is true, then there must be an answer, one yet to be provided, as to why students in the United States score so poorly as compared to students in other countries.[17] Why do our students fare so poorly regarding their knowledge of factual content?

Keeping in mind that internationally normed tests are about *subject-matter content*, one should not overlook the teacher evaluation circumstance described here. As was stated, teachers are not, and cannot be, evaluated with regard to their *subject-matter content* knowledge because their principals are not able to know what good content might be in any but a very few of the subjects tested. Not in any way the fault of their own, principals simply *cannot know* what they *need to know* to perform real subject-matter content knowledge delivery. They are victims of *ineptitude* in this aspect of teacher evaluation.

The ineptitude of principals, that of not being competent to evaluate their teachers' command of subject matter, is not acknowledged by most people associated with the evaluation of teachers. Superintendents, principals, and even teachers refrain from referencing this inconvenient truth. Instead, everyone directs their collective focus to not *what* is taught in classrooms, but *how* it is taught: the pedagogy. As will be seen later, teacher evaluation instruments uniformly focus on *how* subjects are taught, not whether or not the subjects taught represent factually true and accurate content teaching, *what* is taught.

One might assume that, since principals are inept to evaluate the truth and accuracy of *what* is taught, they'd surely be better equipped to evaluate the pedagogy, the means by which subjects are taught. Not a good assumption!

THE SCHOOL PRINCIPAL: A COMMAND OF PEDAGOGY?

As was stated earlier, all public school principals are former classroom teachers themselves. They become principals by completing courses of study in university colleges of education. After completing these courses, and meeting the principal-certification standards in the states wherein they work, they become principals. As principals, these former teachers have now become the authority figures judging the teaching abilities of their former colleagues. But are they qualified to perform this task?

In order to judge the quality of a teaching performance, a principal must *know* what quality teaching *is*. Therefore, it is reasonable to expect that those teachers aspiring to become principals would be selected from the ranks of only those who were high-quality teachers. But how do university principal-training program professors know the teachers applying to become principals were good teachers? The fact is that they do not know.

Teachers applying for principal-training programs typically submit letters of recommendation from previous supervisors, their principals. But while these letters ostensibly speak to their teaching abilities, they are *meaningless* in terms of identifying good teachers from bad teachers. Beyond the legal limitations, those that preclude principals from revealing a teacher's personnel-file information, the principals writing these letters lack the qualifications needed to assess teaching expertise.

Data from the Detroit Public Schools portray a very interesting situation, one seeming to show the ineptitude of the teachers, the principals who evaluate them, or perhaps both.

In 2015, the Detroit Public Schools, for the fourth straight time, scored the lowest among big-city schools in mathematics and reading.[18] In the 2017 National Assessment of Educational Progress, Detroit's eighth-graders were the least proficient among the 27 largest urban school districts. Only 5 percent scored "proficient" in mathematics, and 7 percent scored "proficient" in reading.[19]

However, during the 2015 time period, 79 percent of Detroit teachers were rated as "highly effective" and 17 percent were rated "effective" by their principals. These numbers represent 96 percent of all teachers in the school system.[20] What seems to be displayed by these data is that virtually all the teachers are, supposedly, good teachers. There's just one problem with this: These teachers are not producing good results, i.e., well-educated students. One might see a bit of an incongruity here: How can supposedly good teachers, 79 percent of whom are rated "highly effective," be producing such poorly educated students?

Clearly, letters of recommendation from principals are not very good measures of a teacher-candidate's teaching ability, be it good or bad. But this is about the only criterion university college of education professors have at their disposal to assess the teaching abilities of those seeking entrance to their principal-training programs. And it is a very poor means of assessment indeed! As a result, it's a come one, come all process of admittance. The result is that many who become principals may not know much about good teaching themselves but will soon be in positions whereby they will evaluate it in others.

A WAY OUT OF THE WOODS: WE CAN'T DO *THAT* . . . SO LET'S DO *THIS*

School principals in the United States are confronted with an unresolvable conundrum. They are told that they must evaluate their teachers' performances so as to assure parents that their children are receiving excellent teaching. But what constitutes "excellent teaching"? Is it what the students learn, or is it how they are taught? Either way, principals are inept to fulfill their assigned responsibility to *know* because of their own deficits of knowledge in *both* areas.

School districts across the country address this on-the-ground reality in a fairly uniform way. School district people divert the teacher evaluation discussion away from a *substance* issue, content knowledge, to a *behavioral* issue, pedagogical process. Everyone involved recognizes, whether or not they acknowledge it, that principals are inept to evaluate teachers' content knowledge, and whether or not it is taught accurately and truly. But there is another area wherein principals might be able to fare better: the realm of teachers' behaviors, the things they do in teaching their content. This, not so much a black/white issue, might prove more useful.

With a great degree of *conformity*, schools across the country have resorted to adopting measures of teacher effectiveness that largely center on teachers' *behaviors* in the classroom, not the *content* taught in the classroom. While methodologies differ from state to state, they all exorcise virtually any element that would call upon their principals to possess skill sets they cannot possibly have, i.e., subject content knowledge. In place of content knowledge, these systems insert *process* knowledge. It's a sort of diversionary strategy, something akin to "look at this shiny thing over here!" It's a kind of sleight-of-hand, one that diverts attention. But as will become clear, it merely diverts attention from one form of ineptitude to another form of ineptitude!

As has been discussed, if it is true that principals are no more competent in process than they are in product (pedagogy versus content knowledge), at least they can be made to *appear* competent in one of the two: pedagogy. And in so doing, principals can all learn, together, what good teaching is supposed to *look like*. The underpinning mindset is that all good teaching, regardless of the subject matter being taught, *looks* pretty much the same from classroom to classroom. As such, if a principal knows what the benchmarks are, how good teaching is supposed to *look*, that principal can evaluate any teacher in any subject.

Those districts that have the financial resources to do so, enough dollars in their budgets, hire outside *experts* to show their principals how to evaluate their teachers via these newly designed evaluation yardsticks called *rubrics*. The experts define and explain to the principals what they are to look for in teachers' behaviors, the *right ways* of teaching—how it should *look*. Again, it doesn't matter the subject taught, recognition of good teaching is dependent upon a common core of observable behaviors that all good teachers engage. The experts tell principals what they are and how to recognize them when they see them.

These new measuring sticks (rubrics) for teacher evaluation are attended by a substantial volume of what might be called "education-speak," ostentatious words and phrases that tend to make the simple appear complex. And these rubrics are very *action-specific*. They appear designed so as to allow for easy recognition of *behaviors*, those to be evaluated for their presence or absence. And they are expansive. While teacher behaviors in the classroom are part of the evaluative process, *student* and *parent* behaviors are a part as well.

Above all, it is a one-size-fits-all approach! All teachers, regardless of the subject they teach, are evaluated via the same *rubrics*. While it is obvious that subjects differ, as chemistry differs from French, this fact seems to have escaped the rubric writers. Could it be, perhaps, that the teaching of different subjects might be done differently, evidenced via different pedagogical practices that teachers might engage in their teaching? Might different subjects require different kinds of teaching? Can all subjects, and teachers, then be evaluated via the very same rubrics? The "experts" say they can.

If this kind of one-size-fits-all philosophy of teaching doesn't quite make sense to you, it shouldn't! If you believe that people learn different things differently, and that they engage different kinds of thinking processes while doing so, you are correct. If you then conclude that these different kinds of learning might require differing kinds of thinking, resulting in the need for differing teaching, you are also correct.

In his *Tactics for Thinking* teacher's manual, Dr. Robert Marzano explains how this works:

> The teacher must come between the student and the content, framing the learning situation in such a way as to improve the student's knowledge of content and explicitly reinforce the skills necessary to learn the content.
>
> A basic assumption of this program is that you cannot separate the teaching of thinking from the teaching of content. You must practice thinking about something; classroom content is that "something." Similarly, learning content involves the use of complex thinking skills. **Thinking and content are inextricably linked.** As a

result, the teaching of thinking skills as described in *Tactics* has the effect of improving a student's knowledge of content.[21] (emphasis mine)

Dr. Marzano goes on to list several different kinds of thinking skills, those that have different applications as they may relate to learning in different subject areas. And most importantly, he describes the specific tactics that teachers should engage in teaching these thinking skills, those skills students need to know in order to learn unique bits of information in specific subject domains. Some of these are "pattern recognition, extrapolation, examination of value, concept development, analogical reasoning, and synthesizing."[22]

Clearly, if thinking and content are *inextricably linked* as Dr. Marzano suggests, then a one-way-to-teach approach to evaluating teachers, wherein principals look for teachers to use the *same* strategies in their teaching regardless of the subjects they are teaching, is a badly flawed approach. It is a rubrics game, one that no one can win—least of all the students!

THE RUBRICS GAME:
ONE SIZE FITS ALL

As most states in the United States have adopted standards for teacher evaluation that are largely similar in content, one state's approach is used here. This state is Colorado. The Colorado Department of Education has established teacher evaluation *rubrics* that each school district is *required* to implement. Schools are required to apply these measurement rubrics in the evaluation of their teachers, reporting the results to the Colorado Department of Education at the end of the school year. And while districts may make minor adjustments, the data submitted must conform to the criteria set forth in the state document. This document contains five "quality standards," these collectively forming the bases for teacher evaluation in the state:

Quality Standard I: Teachers demonstrate mastery of and pedagogical expertise in the content they teach. The elementary teacher is an *expert* in literacy and mathematics and is knowledgeable in all other content that he or she teaches (e.g. science, social studies, arts, physical education, or world languages). The secondary teacher has knowledge of literacy and mathematics and is an *expert* in his or her content endorsement area(s).

Quality Standard II: Teachers establish a safe, inclusive and respectful learning environment for a diverse population of students.

Quality Standard III: Teachers plan and deliver effective instruction and create an environment that facilitates learning for their students.

Quality Standard IV: Teachers reflect on their practice.

Quality Standard V: Teachers demonstrate leadership.[23] (emphasis mine)

Taken together, these five standards form the basis for achieving a comprehensive evaluation of a teacher's effectiveness. But as was shown earlier, principals are incapable of evaluating the "mastery" of content of their teachers, that referenced in Quality Standard I. This area of teacher expertise cannot be evaluated/assessed by principals because of their lack of content knowledge that is necessary to assess it.

THE CONTENT TEACHERS TEACH

In order for a principal to assess content (subject-matter) *mastery*, the principal must be a subject-content master. However, as was described earlier, principals are not, and cannot be, subject-content masters. It would be impossible for a principal to be an expert, a so-called *polymath*, in every subject taught in the school. And while common sense would dictate that a "subject expertise" *should* be a standard for assessing teaching quality, a quality all teachers should be expected to possess, nowhere in the "Quality Standard" is there provided any *academically valid* means for a principal to know if the standard is being met.

When asked whether or not the school district principals could evaluate the subject-matter content, given that none had expertise in any of the subjects, one central office administrator in the Denver metropolitan area responded, "Our principals know what good content teaching looks like!" While sounding reasonable, this response is really quite silly!

Content knowledge cannot be measured by its *appearance*, what it "looks like." Content knowledge can be measured only by what it *objec-*

tively is. It is only measured by what it "sounds like." Good content "sounds like" a coherent and cogent narrative, one whose words accurately express cognitively accurate content. It's not about what it "looks like" at all! A taken-from-life example shows how this is true.

In the late 1800s, German embryologist Ernst Haeckel, a staunch advocate of Charles Darwin's evolutionary theories, presented his "ontogeny recapitulates phylogeny" thesis to the scientific community.[24] He proposed that the development of an organism (a human baby in his thesis) displays all the intermediate forms of its ancestors throughout the evolution of the species. Its embryological development, its ontogeny, would duplicate (recapitulate) the evolutionary development of its ancestors, its phylogeny.

As an example, Haeckel referenced the embryological development of a human fetus (baby). At different stages of its development, this fetus would display vestiges of the anatomical structures found in lower-form animal species. For example, the fetus would display rudimentary gill slits, those found in mature fishes, at one early stage in its in-utero embryological development, those later to disappear as the fetus continues in its development. In promoting his theory, Haeckel produced a substantial number of drawings in support of his thesis.

After some considerable debates in the fields of both biology and politics, Haeckel's theory was debunked by other scientists of the time. But Haeckel's theory still remains known to many to this day and is still believed to be true by some. It has been reported that some biology teachers still cite Haeckel's work as they teach Darwinian evolution in their classrooms. But wouldn't a principal *know* that these teachers, those propounding Haeckel's thesis, were teaching a fallacy in place of accurate science?

Most people, including school principals, have likely never heard of Ernst Haeckel or his "ontogeny recapitulates phylogeny" theory. But a presentation of this theory, accompanied with some very graphic and intuitively convincing drawings, would likely convince them of its veracity, and its rightful place in teaching evolutionary theory in a biology class. School principals, lacking knowledge of the subject being taught, would be fooled by an artful, yet specious, teaching performance. This teacher *looked like* a good teacher. Good job!

In this situation, what the teaching performance "looked like" was not an accurate representation of what it, in fact, was! It was a very *poor* teaching performance, because it taught falsehood in the place of scientifically accurate truth. But the principal wouldn't know . . . couldn't know. "Our principals know what good teaching looks like" fails to provide any rationale for evaluating the teaching of accurate and true content information, although the teaching *process* may appear quite acceptable.

While this is but one example, suffice it to say that myriad examples of this form of confused subject-matter teaching can, and likely do, take place in the public schools today. And principals cannot know if or when it is occurring, by being present to see the teacher teach. They are inept to do so. In this situation, what the principal sees is not what the students get. The principal *sees* a teacher to be teaching accurate content, but the students *get* inaccurate content. And some of that inaccurate content, that received by the students, will resurface again when these students respond to an item on a nationally normed test. Could it be that, at least partially, this is why American students fare so poorly on international testing data comparisons with other countries?

To be fair, there will be some school principals who, when asked about this, will admit that they do not possess the content skills to know whether or not accurate and true content is being taught by their teachers. In making this admission, some will submit that they, absent this ability, just "do the best they can." Others, like the central-office administrator referenced earlier, will default to a discussion about the teaching *process*—the observable classroom *behaviors* of their teachers. They will talk about what teaching "looks like," not about what it "is."

But the fact remains, the so-called elephant in the room, that *no* principals are *subject-matter competent* to the extent that they can judge the subject-matter competence of their teachers. How could they be? As stated earlier, it would be humanly impossible for any person to have the intellectual expertise in all the subjects taught in today's middle or high schools, or even in the elementary grades.

As is apparent, Quality Standard I, the *subject-content* standard, is completely outside the reach of school principals. Representing the core essence of education, students' content learning, the inability of principals to meet this standard's expectations is the Achilles' heel of teacher evaluation practices in the public schools today. And while the other "quality standards" may address other issues germane to determining the overall quality of a teaching performance, they cannot compensate for this fundamental deficiency.

THE PEDAGOGY TEACHERS EMPLOY

Briefly defined again, the subjects teachers teach are called the *content*, and the manner in which they teach them is called the *pedagogy*—the actual methods, strategies, or varied practices used to teach the subjects. A biology teacher may have students working in a laboratory, having a hands-on experience with the subject matter presented. They might be using compound microscopes in a unit on entomology, the study of insects. Another teacher might be presenting a lecture about the historical sequence of events leading up to World War II. These two different subjects would, by necessity, require that the teachers teach them differently, one employing a laboratory demonstration and the other an oral narration.

These two teachers will have adopted different teaching strategies, pedagogical approaches, to teach their subject content. Typically, as in this example, the pedagogy a teacher selects is determined by the nature of the content to be taught. Intrinsic in this selection is the understanding that the ease of subject learning by students varies from subject to subject. Not all subjects are learned with equal ease or difficulty. They need to be *taught* differently, essentially because they are *learned* differently. As Dr. Marzano portrays in his *Tactics for Thinking* strategies, different subjects require different thinking. And as thinking is the route to learning, teaching should reflect different routing as well.

In the teaching strategies of Dr. Marzano's *Tactics for Thinking* previously referenced, the biology teacher might utilize the "pattern recognition" tactic to show students how insects all have exoskeletons, the hard outer covering of their soft internal organs. Other patterns of their anatomy might be cited as well. By contrast, the history teacher might ask students to use the "examinations of value" tactic in forming their conclusions about the events leading up to World War II. Different teaching strategies are applied for different venues of learning.

This differentiation in the teaching strategies teachers select, for teaching different subjects, raises an important question, that about the manner in which they are evaluated by their principals. It is this: If teachers select differing teaching strategies because they know that students learn different subjects via different pathways, shouldn't teachers be evaluated differently from one another, on the basis of the subjects they are teaching?

Because they are teaching unique subjects through uniquely different teaching strategies, how can they all be judged using the same rubrics, ones that require principals to look for specific behaviors that apply to all teachers regardless of subjects being taught? In other words, if students learn different subjects *differently*, and teachers therefore teach different subjects *differently*, then why aren't teachers evaluated *differently*?

Ironic as it may seem, all teachers are subjected to the same evaluation standards/rubrics. The checklists for behaviors, both teacher behaviors and student behaviors, are identical for all teachers and students regardless of the subject matter being taught. For example, in Quality Standard 2 in the heretofore referenced evaluation system, teachers (*all* teachers) are graded on whether or not "all students participate in class activities." Also via this standard, students (*all* students) are expected to "engage in collaborative learning and group processes" and to "actively engage in classroom activities."[25] But *all* students do not learn in the same way! It's about those "individual differences" that teachers tell parents about!

Dr. Benjamin Carson, currently the secretary of the US Department of Housing and Urban Development, and previously the director of pediatric neurosurgery at Johns Hopkins Hospital, found that he did not learn well by sitting in classrooms. He was not one to learn by *participating* or being *actively engaged* by the teachers. When he entered medical school at the University of Michigan, Dr. Carson came to the realization that he did not learn in traditional ways. So he took what some might consider extraordinary measures. He did not attend classes, but spent his time reading and reviewing lecture notes, those others who attended classes provided him, for a small fee.[26] In this scenario, Dr. Carson's "individually different" learning style is an example of why the one-size-fits-all teacher evaluation *rubrics* are a bad idea!

Another example of the limitations of the one-size-fits-all methodology comes to us as an exceptionally gifted teacher, the late Jaime Escalante. Those who knew him well, both former students and teachers, say that the movie depicting his career, *Stand and Deliver*, portrays a

very accurate representation of both who he was and *how he taught*.
Escalante taught mathematics at Garfield High School in East Los Angeles in the 1980s. He taught a street-wise group of kids, not academi-
cians by reputation. And his teaching techniques, geared to address the
uniqueness of his students, were not pedagogies that would be lauded
by the Quality Standards referenced earlier.

In one scene from *Stand and Deliver*, Escalante is seen calling a
student "finger man." He calls another "net-head" and routinely refers
to his students as "burros." He makes fun of one male student for the
tattoos the student brandishes on his knuckles, another for his haircut.[27]
Not adhering to commonly accepted *standard* pedagogies, still Escalante was an excellent teacher! And while he was not "celebrating diversity" when he made fun of the differences he observed in his students,
somehow he related to them well and they learned!

What both Dr. Ben Carson's and Jaime Escalante's stories suggest is
that students learn in vastly different ways. This principle, one with
which most principals would be in agreement, should have implications
for how they evaluate their teachers. Other than the requirement that
all content they teach be accurate and true, teachers should be afforded
the freedom to teach in different ways, ways that do not conform to
one-size-fits-all evaluative narratives so commonly imposed by teacher
evaluation instruments, the heretofore referenced *rubrics*, in use today.
The irony here is that, while virtually everyone in public education
today espouses the "individual differences" and the "celebrate diversity"
rhetoric, they all seem to miss the point they preach for teaching and
the evaluation of teaching.

Not only do the "Quality Standards" place principals and teachers in
a one-size-fits-all evaluation context, they also require both to participate in measuring that which cannot be measured. Some of these rubrics present another problem. Principals, sitting in classrooms, cannot
know whether or not some of the Quality Standards rubrics have been
achieved, and the teachers they are evaluating will likely not know either! Some are simply unknowable. Two examples portray this unknow-
ability:

> Quality Standard II: Families and significant others: discuss student
> performance with the teacher participating in school-based activ-
> ities

Quality Standard III: Students: self-assess on a variety of skills and concepts assume ownership for monitoring their progress assume ownership for setting learning goals[28]

While both of these might be seen as good concepts, it is questionable that they should be included in a teacher evaluation assessment process. Two fundamental questions, if asked, would seem to render these two teacher evaluation criteria meaningless:

1. How could any principal reasonably be expected to know whether or not any of these behaviors of students, parents, or significant others, are taking place or have taken place in the past?
2. Assuming that these behaviors of students, parents, and significant others *are* taking place, how are teachers, in any *actionable* way, somehow responsible for them?

What performance standards such as these illustrate is that those who write them appear motivated to make teachers responsible for the attainment of virtually every possible educational outcome regardless of whether or not they are, or even could be!

The end result of "educators" inserting these kinds of *rubrics-rubbish* into teacher evaluation processes is that the structure of the process becomes little more than an ideologically constructed agglomeration of evaluative compost. But these so-called *evaluation* rubrics are neither positively written nor achievable student learning outcomes: those that can be *measured* by principals. And it is not as though school principals do not recognize them as such. A conversation with almost any principal, any willing to risk complete candor, reveals that they merely "check the boxes" to give the state officials what they demand in order to remain in compliance with state teacher evaluation requirements.

Teachers too know how the game is played. They do not take these statewide, and district-adopted, evaluation criteria to be much more than a periodic obligatory nuisance with which they must show the appropriate degree of forbearance—until it's over! Few would candidly assert that these rubrics portend a truly meaningful measurement of their teaching ability, or overall state of their work-related professionalism. For perhaps too many teachers and their principals, it is a form of *education theater* they must endure on a yearly basis.

But why does it continue in this way, virtually unchanged from year to year? Why do principals, their teachers, and the rest of the education coterie membership sustain and advance such an ineffective fraud over time? The answer is that it *does* produce a result. And it is one that, if not subject to scrutiny, sends a positive message to all concerned: "We are accurately and effectively evaluating teachers!" While it is a feel-good experience to all in the education coterie, it also seems to sell well to parents.

But notwithstanding the reams of paperwork and education babble generated, this is an activity predicated upon a false narrative . . . a fraudulent one! Why it continues unabated is a discussion that hinges upon several issues, not the least of which are teacher shortages, union controls, and weak and/or nonexistent leadership at the local public school level. All of these favor the system in place to remain in place, accommodating yearly *tweaking* by those in positions to do so, but resulting in no substantive changes. The "if it ain't broke don't fix it" attitude, while observably not accurate when applied to teacher evaluation, still remains the maxim advocated by all in the education coterie.

STUDENTS' TEST RESULTS: USING BAD DATA . . . BUT SPARINGLY!

Many in the coterie seem inordinately enamored with the matter of "diversity," but it is the very diversity virtue they promote that renders students' test results ineffective, even misleading, in measuring teacher effectiveness. Anyone knowing anything about a classroom of students would know that these young people bring a wide variety of abilities, motivations, and other uniquely personal characteristics to school every day. Every day they bring different packages of these to their class-rooms. As a result, they all learn differently, uniquely, as dictated by their uniquely different personal circumstances.

The things that students bring to school each day, their own personal baggage, are things that will affect their ability to learn on any given day. Are they hungry or well nourished? Are they alert or tired? Is their focus sharp or distracted? Are they happy or sad? Are they physically strong or weak? Are their bodies healthy and pain free, or unhealthy and suffering? Did they depart a one-parent home or a two-parent home? Are they psychologically secure or insecure? Also, could anyone believe that they all arrived with the same innate abilities to learn? In other words, did every student arrive at school, every day, in possession of the *identical mental machinery* to learn as every other student? Are their IQ measures of intelligence all equal?! These are just a few of the issues that comprise their *diversity* from each other as they take their classroom seats each morning.

Do those who advance student testing as an accurate measure of teacher effectiveness not understand the impact that these issues have upon their learning, *despite* the quality for teaching they receive in their classrooms? Some would preface their testing-approach advocacy by saying "All things being equal . . ." But as can be seen, all things are *not* equal. The students are the "things" here, and they are certainly not equal when it comes to each one's ability to perform well on any given day, perhaps on the day a standardized test is given.

Some university professors of education, those who advocate for the use of student testing as teacher-effectiveness measurements, say that they recognize these variances and that they take "them into consideration." They suggest that student test scores are used sparingly, as just *one part* of a teacher's evaluation. But is that a reasonable response, especially coming from a university professor? Why would a teacher take comfort in knowing that just a *part* of his/her evaluation was based upon an invalid criterion regardless of how *sparingly* it was applied? Why include something, even sparingly, if it is prima facie *wrong*?

University professors are typically engaged in research and teaching. In both, they inform their work through the use of statistical measurement. In statistical measurement, the effect of a treatment is evaluated by applying two measurements, *validity* and *reliability*. A treatment is said to be valid if it produces the result it intended to produce. It is reliable if that result is replicated, consistently, over time. If a treatment is not valid, does not produce the desired effect, its reliability measurement becomes inconsequential.

If student testing is not a *valid* measure, unable to render the result it intends (measuring teaching ability in this case), why should it be applied at all, no matter how much or little it is applied? In this case, professors' assertion that student testing is used sparingly becomes irrelevant, just as it would be irrelevant to be concerned about the reliability of any treatment once it has proven ineffective. Using bad data to evaluate teacher effectiveness is a seriously flawed endeavor, notwith-standing that this activity receives the imprimatur of some university professors of education.

It should be noted here that most parents would likely not have a grasp of the statistical paradigms of "validity" and "reliability," those that school people have: superintendents, principals, and university professors. Not having these conceptual understandings, parents cannot recognize that the use of student test scores to evaluate teaching perfor-mance is a badly flawed endeavor. Even if they suspect such, the asser-tion by the school people that these scores are used *sparingly* is likely to allay any concerns they might have. But the school people *do* under-stand! They know that using an invalid measurement criterion is not mitigated in its negative consequences, bad measurement data, just because it is used sparingly. This is another example of the *obfuscation* educators engage in the matter of teacher evaluation . . . in this case purposefully.

MISSION CREEP:
SOME *NEW* STANDARDS FOR TEACHER EVALUATION

Those watching the goings-on in public education these days have likely noticed that many unusual things have found their way into the school curriculum, things that seem to have popped up almost overnight. Those who still hold to the belief that the three R's are the foundation of good schooling may find themselves scratching their heads at some of these. Are these new approaches really attached in some meaningful way to student learning, or are they the hallmarks of ideological group-think—a politically correct ideology of the education coterie?

One criterion today deemed an example of *quality education* calls upon teachers to tailor their teaching to conform to a fairly new ideolog-ical precept, "diversity." For anyone unfamiliar with *the latest and greatest* in public education "thinking" today, they need to be updated in the contemporary belief that "diversity" appears to be a public school priority. "Celebrate diversity!" is heard everywhere in public education. The word appears virtually everywhere in educational discourse, and particularly at the universities charged with the responsibility for training new teachers. And it is ensconced in local-level teacher evaluation processes as well.

Teachers are graded upon their ability to "create a classroom environment in which *diversity* is used to further student learning," upon "using instructional approaches and materials that reflect *diverse* backgrounds and experiences," and "creating a classroom environment which values *diverse* perspectives," and their display of "respect for *individual differences*."[29] This gives a wholly new meaning to what teachers used to refer to as *individual differences*.

While teachers have always recognized that their students differ, one from the other, they have typically engaged these difference characteristics in their teaching in ways that make positive uses of them. A teacher recognizing that a student can learn a new concept best by comparing it to an old one might use the strategy of analogy to teach that student. However, nowhere in this student-teacher relationship does the student somehow become elevated in status just because he/she has a *different* learning style—a *diverse* one. Teachers have not, in the past, become motivated to acknowledge such a condition as deserving adulation accruing to its mere existence, somehow now demanding honor and *celebration* for their mere existence. But, of course, this is not the kind of *diversity* that school people now celebrate!

"Diversity," now taken to mean mostly social behaviors that are culturally aberrant, is but one example of what can be seen as a relentless form of mission creep in public schools today, and what now falls under the purview of the school principal's evaluation duties. Most of these are not learning-related matters, but are merely social-science experiments that have become insinuated into the public school curriculum. And none of these, as was described earlier, are reviewed or evaluated by school principals. They are those parts of "schooling" that "fly under the radar."

But what can parents do? If they are not in agreement with either what is taught, how it's taught, or their students' learning progress, what can they do? Of course they can go to the school and complain, but if there is no satisfaction to be had there, can they take legal action against the school? Is there anything that parents can do to stem assault on the intellectual integrity of their schools? Could they, perhaps, sue?

EDUCATION MALPRACTICE?
CAN PARENTS SUE?

Public schools are perpetrating a *fraud* on the public via asserting that their agents, school principals, have the ability to effectively evaluate the teaching performances of their teachers. As has been shown in the previous pages, principals are inept to perform this function; thus, the assertion is observably false. Additionally, members of what has been called the education coterie consort with school principals in supporting and maintaining this false narrative. While not acting in any conspiratorial manner, but nonetheless acting cooperatively, they jointly obfuscate in the matter of providing evidence that the result they promise is being achieved, that result being the accurate and true evaluation of teachers.

As this is being written, the news media are reporting that a woman was killed by a driverless car in Arizona.[30] This vehicle, being tested on the streets of Tempe by the Uber company, struck and killed a woman crossing the street. When the event occurred, a "vehicle operator" was in the driver's seat, but the car was being operated in "autonomous mode." While this event is still being investigated, it is almost certain that the family of the deceased woman will have access to the application of statute law as it applies to this incident. They will likely sue.

While the above case displays clearly that legal action can, and should, be brought when the actions of one party injure another, such is not the case when educators are found not to be delivering what they promised. While educators promise the delivery of a product and the means to assure that it is delivered (quality teaching and a viable teacher evaluation process) they cannot be sued for their failure to perform. In short, they cannot be sued for *malpractice*, for failing to deliver that which they said they would deliver.

Educators (teacher, principals, superintendents, and boards of education) cannot be held liable for failing to educate because the process of educating students contains far too many elements of variability, many outside the control of educators.

> A legal definition of educational malpractice is yet to be codified, but the term can be assumed to involve professional negligence or the failure to provide services that can reasonably be expected. Unlike many other professional services, however, education relies on the active participation of the client—the student—and depends to a

great extent on factors outside the school's control. Largely for this reason, courts have been reluctant to find schools, school officials, or school employees sufficiently responsible to be held liable for student failures to learn, even when parents can show they have been misled regarding their children's progress.[31]

The system of jurisprudence in the United States does not see fit to hold educators accountable for assuring that students will become educated through their actions, and justifiably so. As the above *legal* opinion suggests, the results educators can achieve in their students' learning are subject to the influence of too many factors that lie outside their purview and control. As was detailed earlier, students come to school with their own personal *baggage*, the things that predispose them to learn well, or not.

The courts recognize that the *baggage* students bring to school with them, those things that lie "outside the school's control," provide sufficient cause so as to not hold the school liable for students' failure to learn. In a word, they find it unfair to hold teachers accountable for things they cannot control. One might wonder why university professors, and their coterie colleagues, see fit to do what the courts refuse to do. They seem to have no problem holding teachers accountable for the testing results their students achieve, evaluating them by using these scores as measures of their teachers' expertise.

THE EDUCATION COTERIE: RETURNING TO GEORGE ORWELL'S *1984*?

The Coterie Defined

The *education coterie* is a loosely knit agglomeration of people and organizations associated with the public schools. At the local level it is comprised of *professional* educators: superintendents of schools, ancillary central-office administrators, school principals, and others associated with public education in some fashion. Others in this group are university departments of education, local boards of education, teachers' unions, prominent writers in the field of education, governmental departments of education, educational organizations, and education-related activist groups.

Some of these act within the walls of school buildings, but many others exert their influence from outside. These people and groups comprise the structural essence of the education coterie, a body of influence that substantially impacts *everything* that takes place in today's public schools. And while perhaps not a commonly used term in today's vernacular, coterie aptly describes this grouping: "Coterie" is "a small group of people with shared *interests* or *tastes*, especially one that is *exclusive of other people.*"[32] (emphasis mine)

The education coterie is a bureaucracy of bureaucracies. As such, it may be responsive to subtle forms of *tweaking*, but certainly not substantial changing. Tweaking might be seen by way of subtle manipulations in content presentations, but not of the content presented! It would be like asking a dyed-in-the-wool Ford *car guy* to buy a Chrysler. He *might* consider a four-door Ford over his current two-door, but he'd certainly not consider buying a Chrysler! This is the education coterie—willing to accept minor modifications, but not much in the way of substantial change. Philosophy is largely animated by ideology, and the ideology is fixed. It is politically liberal, definitively not conservative, in both form and function.

How the Coterie Functions

The people and/or organizations comprising this group are in no way acting in a conspiratorial manner, nor do they aspire to secrecy in what they do. While some of what they promote is antithetical to the historical foundational principles of public education, they make no secret of their beliefs or desires, or programs for changing public education to incorporate them. And while public education is historically founded upon the premise that the *public* determines its schooling, the coterie is observably resistant to public control. Coterie members uniformly conform to an observably liberal form of *group-think.*

The education coterie is in the forefront in manifesting a philosophical mindset that has taken hold of 21st-century political and social thinking in the United States. In advancing its agenda, it places *group* interests ahead of *individual* interests, and many of their interests emanate from the political left. An example is their conformed advocacy for

LGBT welfare interests, as a group, ahead of students' individual welfare interests. And their methods are not new. It's all about changing, and then assiduously managing, the vocabulary!

Aside from the pervasive influence of *political correctness* that has swept the nation in recent years, perhaps the most powerful weapon in the arsenal of the education coterie is what George Orwell titled "newspeak" in his 1949 novel, *1984*. Orwell describes the goal of newspeak succinctly in his essay, "Politics and the English Language": "If thought corrupts language, language can also corrupt thought."[33] In *1984*, the goal is to reorient people's thinking by changing the meanings of the words they use, resultantly changing the culture in which they live.

How the Coterie Influences

In promoting social-experiment agendas, whatever may be their origins, today's education coterie utilizes the tactics of yesteryear. Coterie member organizations conform in parroting a common core of word usage, Orwellian *newspeak*, to underpin the ideological mindsets of the societal changes they seek. A key strategy is an endless repetition of what they wish people to believe. They have good reason to utilize this approach. It works!

"Repetition: When people hear or see a belief repeated and reinforced by the *selective* presentation of facts, they believe it more strongly. The entire concept of advertising is based upon this tendency."[34] (emphasis mine) *Selective* means that some salient facts will be left out of the discussion, those that are not supportive of the narrative being repeated. A few coterie examples show how this is accomplished.

The NASSP (National Association of Secondary School Principals) says that all public school staff members should "use the student's preferred name and pronoun which is a sign of respect to the student and affirms his or her gender identity."[35] The NEA (National Education Association), the teachers' union, says, "Students have a right to be called by their preferred name and pronoun" and "Institutions should accept a student's assertion of the student's gender identity and not require any particular substantiating evidence."[36]

The NAESP (National Association of Elementary School Principals) is in lockstep with their colleagues at the NASSP. Under the guise of "supporting transgender students," they advance the agenda of organizations such as the Gender Spectrum, which advocates the position that "male" and "female" are inadequate categorizations. Gender Spectrum people say that gender binary is nothing but a "simplistic notion."[37]

NOTE: It is interesting that, just up until a few years ago, the term "gender" was not in broad usage in American culture. For those who took Latin as a high school subject a few decades ago, the term referenced three distinct contexts: masculine, feminine, and neuter. The term "gender" was a reference to "sex," but not a term interpreted beyond the meanings of "male," "female," or neither . . . "asexual." Today, LGBTQI devotees would have everyone believe that "gender" is not *one distinct* "sex," but a fluid concept that describes many different *forms* of sex. Is it likely that those teaching Latin today will be obligated to change the structure of the language they teach? Latin has, for a very long time, been referred to as "dead language." *That* would surely bring it back to life!

The CHSAA (Colorado High School Activities Association) governs all public school athletics in Colorado. It says that all school staff members should "Use correct names/pronouns according to the student's self-identification, and permit the student to dress according to gender identity or expression" and to "allow restroom and locker room access consistent to gender identity."[38]

The ASCD (Association for Supervision and Curriculum Development) openly lobbies educators to accept one-way sexual identity thinking as the educational construct all *must* support. Ellen Kahn, in an article written in its publication *Educational Leadership*, asserts:

> The important takeaway is that young people are challenging the gender binary notion that one must be either male or female—and it's up to us to allow space for students to tell us and show us who they are, rather than making assumptions on the basis of a name, clothing, voice, or other attributes we typically associate with gender. In other words, *follow your students' lead on how they self-identify* and respond by affirming and respecting that identity.[39] (emphasis mine)

Somewhat ironic is that this article appears in a publication titled *Educational Leadership*. Telling principals, and others charged with leading, to merely *follow* (i.e., agree with!) what their students are *doing* is not only silly, but tantamount to a failure to perform their contractual duties of responsible adult supervision. What the ASCD article does not include is that Ellen Kahn is a long-standing member of a national LGBTQ advocacy organization, the Human Rights Campaign, which described itself as "the largest national lesbian, gay, transgender and queer civil rights organization."[40]

And while Canada is several miles to the north, Gender Spectrum and its associates are supportive of Ontario Premier Kathleen Wynne's proposal to remove the terms "mother" and "father" from her government's lexicon.[41] Wynn, the first LGBT premier in Canada, is advancing a cause that may soon be coming to neighborhoods in the United States. Given how easily coterie members adopt LGBT talking points, this is not an unlikely possibility. Keep in mind that local, state, and national governmental figures in this country are coterie members, as is apparently also the circumstance in Canada. The blurring of commonly accepted vocabulary is already in play in America. Some people have taken to reference a man, in a homosexual relationship with another man, as the other man's "wife." Once again, it's about changing and then carefully managing the *vocabulary*!

The Rest of the Story

"Now you know the *rest* of the story!"[42] As described earlier, that's what radio commentator Paul Harvey would enjoy reporting to his audience. He'd begin by telling his listeners a story, perhaps about a news event, that he knew they had likely heard long ago. But now he would fill them in on some behind-the-scenes facts, some things that they didn't get when they first heard the story. And these new revelations would change listeners' views, what he thought they knew when they heard the story for the first time.

The examples of the education coterie's pronouncements just cited all advocate for school persons, teachers, principals, etc., to accept and promote radical social behaviors that are highly questionable on a wide variety of levels, and also damaging at many. While there is yet no long-term assessment, either socially or scientifically, regarding the effects of children deciding that they are the sex other than the one they were born into (those that do exist show that children are substantially damaged![43]), the coterie organizations mentioned herein all, with nearly

100 percent conformity, advocate for a position of unconditional acceptance and support for the transgender phenomenon.

While coterie view-conformity would be warranted if the behaviors advocated were logically consistent and scientifically well founded, this is not the case. As the author of *When Harry Became Sally* (Ryan T. Anderson) suggests, "The claims of transgender activists are confusing because they are philosophically incoherent"[44] and "at the core of the ideology is the radical claim that feelings determine reality."[45]

A more sobering assessment of transgenderism derives from a recently published science-based research paper. It states that 41 percent of people who *identify* as transgender will attempt suicide at some point in their lives, as compared to 4.6 percent of the general population.[46] These are among the data points that likely prompt Dr. Paul McHugh, distinguished professor of psychiatry at the Johns Hopkins School of Medicine, to say, "Think, for example, of the parents whom no one—not doctors, schools, nor even churches—will help to rescue their children from these strange notions of being transgendered and the problematic lives these notions herald."[47]

Why educational organizations such as those cited continue to lobby for actions so harmful to children may be partly explained by the influence of political correctness in the culture today, and the kind of thinking that underpins it: "Postmodern thinkers seek to undermine the very concept of the normative and to obscure the fact that a natural order exists."[48]

What this kind of lockstep coterie positioning portends for public education is a formalized educational process that has become an agent of social-engineering projects, advancing special-interest *group* agendas, with the education and welfare of children no longer the number-one priority. As was shown in chapter 2, some of what is happening in the public schools, when the news media brings it to light, is truly remarkable! People who hear about new school bathroom policies and white privilege classes are beginning to think that they are now living in an alternate universe, or that their schools are! The commonly heard question being asked is, "What does this have to do with my kid's learning math, science . . . whatever?!"

What this means for public education is that quality teaching is getting lost in a sea of alternative-thinking social-engineering projects, and students are the resultant losers. As a result, *principled* leadership, that heretofore accomplished by school principals, has become an endangered species. Living within the milieu of the education coterie renders leading *away* from politically correct orthodoxy highly risky, especially for those in so-called leadership positions such as the school principal. For school principals, exerting leadership that opposes a coterie orthodoxy can result in serious repercussions, not the least of which is reassignment or termination.

The Fruits of Coterie Conformity

Current-day example: For a moment, imagine the firestorm to ensue should a high school principal *disallow* a student's participation on an athletic team on the basis of his/her "transitioning" status. Most common-sense-thinking parents, particularly those having student-athletes participating on the athletic team at issue, would think it a correct decision. But this kind of *leadership, exerted* by a high school principal, would likely result in his/her termination by the school board. The coterie is strong!

A girls' high school wrestling tournament in Texas speaks to this strength. There, a "transitioning" girl, pumped up with anabolic steroids to enable her to become a "he," won a state championship. This result was animated and enabled by policies established by the University Interscholastic League, the Texas state-level high school athletics organization. The student, a biological female at birth, was "transitioning" to become a male. For that purpose, she was being injected with anabolic steroids, to facilitate this "transition."

The University Interscholastic League, the governing body for high school athletics in Texas, provides that steroid usage by high school athletes is prohibited, but with one proviso:

> Both state laws and UIL rules prohibit illegal steroid use during athletic events. State law (Section 33.091 of the Texas Education Code) provides an exception for a steroid that is prescribed by a medical practitioner for a *valid medical purpose.*[49] (emphasis mine)

While it might seem reasonable to ask whether or not enabling gender dysphoria via injecting steroids has a "valid medical purpose," the University Interscholastic League seems to have decided that it does. It also seems to have disregarded the warning, issued by the American College of Pediatricians, that gender-changing drugs administered to their student-athletes have a harmful effect.[50] The president of that organization has stated that transgender ideology, that which enables the University Interscholastic League's policy statement, is tantamount to child abuse.[51] One might wonder why the University Interscholastic League, having no medical or scientific acumen, would arbitrarily ignore the consensus findings of medical doctors, those findings portending great damage to the student-athletes the UIL is supposed to protect.

But where was the high school *principal* in this chain of events in Texas? While he was the front line of defense for his student-athletes, what role did he play in protecting them? Notwithstanding that this story generated substantial national news coverage, no reporting of this story carried any mention of his name or involvement. Was there any leadership exerted by this principal in preventing this chain of events from taking place? Or did he succumb to the prevailing wishes of the education coterie, manifesting through the grossly ill-informed pronouncements of the University Interscholastic League?

As is seen in this wrestling scenario, some outcomes can turn out to be other than desirable. But there is an abundance of *obfuscation* regarding the outcomes achieved by members of the coterie. In the wrestling case cited, the state athletic organization rendered its decision allowing the student to compete, while disregarding scientific findings. While fact-based data were apparently excluded from their decision-making process, the organization advanced the false narrative that it had considered *all* aspects of the situation in reaching its decision. As the evidence presented herein shows, they did not.

A recent Pew Research Center study states that the United States, as compared to dozens of other developed and developing countries, ranks thirty-eighth in measurements of math, science literacy, and other key skills.[52] If these data reflect the true academic achievement of America's young people, perhaps they more so provide a window into the failure in leadership of those directing the educational techniques responsible for these results. Clearly, those in leadership positions, superintendents and principals at the local level, have failed to lead to a very positive result over a wide range of evaluative venues.

The Coterie and Principal Leadership

Some may think that the transgender issue is not important enough to have commanded so much attention in these pages. After all, the topic is teacher evaluation, not sexual preference. Why *so* much on this then? Suffice it to say that this issue is perhaps the most significant issue to impact public education in this, or any other, generation! It incorporates the capacity to affect virtually every aspect of public schooling: school discipline, teacher conduct, interscholastic athletics, the school curriculum, societal social conventions, parental rights, etc. As such, it is a bellwether for principal leadership, a harbinger of the degree to which principals will be able to lead, in *any* area, within their schools. And that includes the most important function: teacher evaluation.

It may appear that the role of the education coterie has been overstated in tying it to the leadership roles principals play in their schools. But what would be missing in this view is the fact that the world of a school principal *is* the world of the coterie. The education coterie circumscribes everything a school principal does. Existentially, the coterie constricts the leadership behaviors of school principals in adherence to a well-understood, and politically correct–conformed, code of conduct.

All coterie members manifest a mindset about educational issues that is essentially identical. Whether about social policy, parent organizational structure, curriculum appropriateness, or teacher evaluation, the policy positions conform to a commonly accepted and promulgated group-think. The coterie, in a word, *proscribes* the behaviors of principals, and particularly those to be avoided, by virtue of its idea of what is proper professional conduct.

But this discussion of the education coterie's effect upon the school principal is not presented as an excuse for principals exerting little to no real leadership in their schools. It is intended to present a description of the existential circumstance that determines the extent of leadership principals can *afford* to engage. As most principals know, there is a range of movement within the proscriptions within which they are expected to operate. Stepping out of this range comes with a high risk for building principals. And in staying "within the lines," their leadership function dwindles.

A building principal electing to exercise leadership through the application of actions not conforming to the school district's established evaluation criteria would be censured, perhaps first by the teachers'-union building representative—a coterie member. More so, a violation of the precepts of *political correctness* in teacher evaluations, those not codified in the rubrics, would likely bring a more emphatic response from the educational establishment. Given the social pressures special-interest activist groups can bring to bear, it would not be unlikely that such an incident could threaten the job security of a principal.

This kind of infraction would likely bring charges from a number of coterie members: the superintendent of schools, local board of education members, state organizations, and even some teachers. Unlike a principal's perceived misstep in a *rubric-related* teacher evaluation matter, being perceived as politically incorrect in teacher evaluation interactivity can bring dire consequences for principals. A "wrong" word or phrase can be lethal to a principal's standing!

What all of this means is that principals are well aware that, while ostensibly hired to be school *leaders*, there are very few areas wherein they can exert *real* and *principled* leadership. Perhaps because of the way in which the position of school principal came into being, not originally requiring a leadership role but merely an administrative one, principals today remain conformed to this role. They remain largely *presiders* over circumstances that exist, not *leaders* moving toward better ones. The "go along to get along" philosophy of day-to-day school administration, promoted and enabled by the education coterie, exerts its influence on building principals, especially those wishing to remain in their positions.

The Coterie and Parents

One might be wondering what role *parents* play in influencing the education coterie, in how it affects their children's schooling. The answer: They have no role! And this, even more than the principal's lack of leadership influence, represents a major failure in public education today. While parents have the greatest investiture in their children, they are the only group left out of the process. More than ever before, parents find themselves disenfranchised from the education of their children. But in fairness, they have chosen this result by their failure to stay *actively* involved in their children's schooling.

Parents are busy with their workplace lives, their social engagements with friends, others in the community, and a variety of things that they choose to engage. Unfortunately, these too often are held as higher priorities than keeping track of what's going on for their children in their schools. And as has been shown, there's a *lot* going on, much of which should be the *first* priority of parents. The days when parents could trust the public schools to look out for their children's safety and best interests are long gone!

But unlike the coterie, formally organized and dedicated to a purpose, parents are not so organized, or not organized at all. While they are many in number, they have no meaningful and influential *group voice*. And as recent experience has shown, while large numbers of students' well-being interests can be ignored, the interests of a powerful group voice (activist group) can have a substantial impact in public schooling. But parents are increasingly seeing their interests and concerns sublimated to the "professional" educators, those who seek to inculcate *their* agendas for educating children in place of the agendas parents wish to see.

John Goodlad, author of the widely celebrated book *A Place Called School*, stated, "Our goal is behavioral change. The majority of our youth still hold to the values of their parents, and if we do not recognize this pattern, if we do not re-socialize them to accept change, our society may decay."[53] While Goodlad made this statement over thirty years ago, those advocating for his beliefs are seeing them becoming an integral part of the public school curriculum today. But while Goodlad apparently believed parental viewpoints to be antiquated, does it follow that they are necessarily wrong? And are the schools to merely *assume* that they are, and then act against them? Apparently this is so.

As is true for many matters in public education, parents find themselves without a voice in this matter, and they know that their school principal will not help them achieve one. Similarly, parents have no voice in the evaluation of the teachers who teach their children. But this can change. There are relatively simple strategies to apply that can result in better outcomes for both. These will be addressed in chapter 4, where solutions to the problems presented in this part are described.

IS THIS ONE A *GOOD* TEACHER . . . IS THIS ONE A BAD TEACHER?
THE QUESTION DEMANDING AN ANSWER

As was stated earlier, the quality of a teaching performance is determined by measuring the degree to which two entities are *observably* evident: (1) accurate knowledge of the subject matter being taught and (2) well-informed methodologies for the teaching of the subject matter. "Observably" is an important reference here in that it is commonly accepted that a teacher's teaching ability lends itself to an evaluation by another person, one said to be *competent* to make such a judgment. In other words, one person can observe another and render a judgment, within a reasonable degree of accuracy, that the teaching was good, bad, mediocre, etc.

It would seem to go without saying that one person can appropriately and effectively evaluate the performance of another, but this mindset is subject to one critical provision: The person doing the evaluating must be competent to do it! An example: If an auto mechanic's ability to install new brake components on an automobile is to be evaluated by another person, the other person must have as much, *or more*, ability to perform that job as the mechanic being evaluated. If the evaluating person is inept in performing brake jobs, no *valid* evaluation is possible. But is teaching different?

Some people would say that teaching, unlike any other act, is so dependent upon the intricate interactivity between the student and the teacher that it cannot be accurately assessed by an outside observer. There's so much *unobservable* mental activity engaged in the process, by both student and teacher, that a straight-line assessment, cause and effect, is virtually impossible. Who could know, for example, what *part* of what a teacher says triggers a learning insight by a student? Can a good student learn from a bad teacher? Can a bad student learn from a good teacher? And is there one way, one best methodology, for teaching *all* students?

The education coterie, those in the educational establishment associated with teacher evaluation, purport to have answers to these questions. First, they would suggest that an observer *can* know what kinds of mental engagement in the student, ostensibly generated by the teacher, will uniformly stimulate a student to gain a learning insight. Second, they would suggest that this process is a one-size-fits-all phenomenon that any good teacher can bring about. There is a *best methodology* for good teaching, and principals can see it when it is happening.

Most in the coterie, some being university professors, further suggest that student learning is *predictably* the result of, caused by, good teaching. If the students learn, the teaching was good! If the students do not learn, then the teaching was not so good. This is the mindset that animates the coterie to inject student testing results, typically on standardized testing, into the teacher evaluation process. While the courts have routinely refused to accept these cause-effect judgments, those in the educational establishment (the coterie) insist on inserting them into the teacher evaluation circumstance.

TEACHING AND EVALUATING TEACHING: THINGS OTHER COUNTRIES DO . . . THAT WE DO NOT

As mentioned, nationally normed international testing shows that students in the United States do not score as well when compared with students in other developed countries. The students in other countries know more of the *information* being tested; they have greater content knowledge than do their US counterparts. Are these students just inherently more intelligent than US students as they enter into their formal schooling? Or is their formal schooling substantially different so as to render them more academically skilled?

It is sufficient to acknowledge that the education systems in other countries, as in Japan for example, are reflections of the cultures of those countries. As such, it would be inappropriate to make one-to-one comparisons of testing results absent a consideration of these differences. But notwithstanding the cultural differences, teachers in Japan teach their students differently than is done in the United States, and these differences have to do with *what* is taught, not so much *how* they teach.

Content knowledge gained is the endgame in Japan, not teaching strategies. For teachers, their success is evidenced by their students learning and retaining information, information that they subsequently are able to display in testing situations such as the nationally normed tests referenced earlier. Teachers in many other countries, again referencing Japan as an example, undergo a greater degree of training in the academic subjects they teach than do their American counterparts. In addition, they face greater challenges in passing the examinations they must successfully pass in order to become teachers.[54] As a result of both, they are more *academically* (subject matter) competent than their US counterparts. Undoubtedly this circumstance has a great deal to do with the training the teachers in Japan receive, as compared to their US counterparts.

The 1983 *Nation at Risk* study addressed the issue of inferior *subject-matter* training in America's teacher-training colleges and universities:

> The teacher preparation curriculum is weighted heavily with courses in "education methods" at the expense of courses in subjects to be taught. A survey of 1,350 institutions training teachers indicated that 41 percent of the time of elementary school teacher candidates is spent in education courses, which reduces the amount of time available for subject matter courses.[55]

A Nation at Risk debuted in 1983 and created a stir in the education community as it shined light upon the inadequate course offerings in university colleges of education across the country. But what was a bad situation over thirty years ago seems to have become only worse since that time. The University of Oregon is but one example of how far afield academic rigor, that which future teachers are expected to possess, has fallen.

At this university, the degree program for an "Education Foundations major" is described as follows: "The purpose of the Education Foundations major is to prepare future professionals in elementary education and related fields who are critical thinkers, well informed about theory and practice, and who possess the knowledge and skills that will enable them to be *change agents* in economically, racially, culturally, and linguistically diverse communities."[56] (emphasis mine). Some course offerings for this degree program are:

EDST 440 PE for Diverse Learners
EDST 111 School and Representation in Film
ES 256 Introduction to Native American Studies
WGS 101 Women, Difference, and Power

WGS 201 Introduction to Queer Studies[57]

While these courses have little if any relevance to academic subject matter, their relevance is certainly in tune with the "change agent" goal cited in the Education Foundations program description. But what *kind* of change is sought via "queer studies" coursework? Parents might justifiably question both the need for, and appropriateness of, elementary teachers seeking this kind of change in their children.

Might not more instruction in mathematics, the sciences, and the English language be a better use of instructional time? The answer could be "No!" if parents worried that their children might get a low "queer studies" grade in international testing, compared to children in other countries. But then they'd have no need for concern, because other countries dedicate their teaching time to mathematics, the sciences, and language—not "queer studies"!

Teachers in other countries, those that outscore US students in national testing measurements, are evaluated on their *academic* strengths, and the degree to which they transmit their subject-matter knowledge to their students. They are evaluated on their ability to produce a *product*, educated students, not so heavily by the *process* by which they seek to produce that product.

While it may not be wise to take our cues in teacher evaluation, or education in general, from other countries, it is short-sighted not to recognize that some of what is accomplished in those countries is laudable. And while the United States may not find a better system for teacher evaluation by looking abroad, educators in the United States should not avert their eyes from the evidence presented herein that the US system is in need of *major* improvements. In short, the teacher evaluation systems currently in place, and the staffing that animates them, are in need of a major reorganization.

GOING FORWARD:
PRINCIPALS CAN'T DO THE JOB . . . SO NOW WHAT?

There currently remain many more questions about teacher evaluation than there are answers, and many make for interesting debates. But the reality on the ground is that parents have a right to ask if the teachers in their children's schools are good, or not good. And as responsible stewards of educating these children, public school officials should have an answer . . . and they do! They say "Yes we can!" The schools say that they *can* tell you, parents, about the quality of the teaching done by our teachers. They state that their school principals have the knowledge and expertise to observe the teachers in their classrooms, and to then make accurate judgments regarding the quality of teaching they have witnessed!

But principals can't! While members of the education coterie (principals, superintendents, school board members, national education organizations, teachers' unions) conform in their agreement that teacher quality can be effectively evaluated by school principals, this is not true. It should be noted that teachers, as a unionized group, are not as lockstep in this view as are others in the coterie. It's not to their bargaining advantage to be such. But they go along, at least tacitly, with the conforming view, to the extent that they participate in their evaluation processes with their evaluators.

Now, with the assertion that principals cannot adequately evaluate their teachers, it is time to address the reasons for their predicament. Their predicament is that they are called upon to do something that they know, and some admit, they cannot perform. Yes, *some* principals admit that they cannot do what their superintendents tell them to do . . . but what are they to do?! They are in the unenviable position "between the rock and the hard place," between what they are told to do and what they know they can't do, and so they make the best of their circumstance.

In fairness to these principals, they *are* doing the best they can. But they can do better if those in the education coterie would help them get to a better place. The first step is recognizing that the *ineptitude, conformity*, and *obfuscation*, that which keeps the status quo in place, has to cease!

There is a large amount of *turf protection* engaged by coterie members, a safety-in-numbers mindset that pervades most bureaucracies that are like it. This must be addressed in order for much of anything to change in public education. And while such change is necessary for public education to escape the group-think that currently defines it, the issue here is how to make positive changes in teacher evaluation processes—those needed so that parents can know that their children have the very best teachers teaching their children.

How to fix what's been described herein as broken . . . that's next!

4

THE WAY WE CAN BE

Toward *Better* Teacher Evaluation

As has been described, there is a great deal that's wrong with the way public school teachers are evaluated today. But merely pointing out what's wrong, in the absence of putting forth suggestions for righting the wrongs, would be telling only half the story about teacher evaluation. It would not include, as was previously referenced, Paul Harvey's *The Rest of the Story*.[1] details—those left-out parts that give meaning to the original story. The original story presented here has been all about poor-quality teacher evaluation systems, what's *wrong* with how public schools evaluate their teachers. What comes next, *the rest of the story*, addresses what was left out of the original story, how to *fix* what's wrong, to make it right.

In many ways, what's wrong with teacher evaluation systems currently in vogue is akin to what Hans Christian Andersen described in his 1837 fairy tale, "The Emperor's New Clothes."[2] In that story, an emperor was convinced by charlatans that they could dress him in some uniquely powerful clothing. This clothing, they told him, could not be seen by people who were either stupid or not fit to see by virtue of their low station in life.

The emperor, not wanting to admit that *he* could not see the clothing they described, not wanting to be thought stupid or unqualified himself, allowed these people to dress him in clothes that, in point of fact, did not exist. The con artists thus pretended to place these magical garments on the emperor while leaving him completely naked. And now the emperor, decked out in what he knew would be a display of his regal nature and intelligence, became the center of attention as he led a procession through town.

In the meantime, the townspeople had heard of the emperor's new clothes, and that only the stupid or unqualified would be unable to see them. Unwilling to admit that they were either, the townspeople wildly praised the clothes they "saw" their emperor wearing as he strode through their midst, until a small boy exclaimed, "But he has nothing on!"

Hearing this, the people began to whisper to one another what the boy had said. Then they all began to shout out that the emperor had nothing on—he was naked! Hearing this, the emperor believed he was reinforced in judging that his subjects were, indeed, stupid. They, he surmised, could not see his magnificent attire because they were *unqualified* to do so, as he'd been told by his deceivers. And so he strode on, proudly convinced that he alone possessed the capacity to see his new clothing, the ability that now distinguished him from his lowly subjects.

The message of this story is clear. Some people, wishing to retain a belief system to which they conformingly subscribe, are willing to pretend that something is true when it is, observably, not true. This is similar to the education coterie's advancing the notion that school principals can, and do, effectively evaluate the teaching performances of their teachers. But as was true with the emperor, their claim is *naked* . . . a false claim. Now all that remains is to suggest how a failed system can be turned into a sound system, finally putting some *real* clothing on the emperor!

FIXING TEACHER EVALUATION SYSTEMS: GETTING PAST "YOU DON'T MESS AROUND WITH JIM!"

In 1972, the late singer-songwriter Jim Croce recorded what was to become a hit single record, "You Don't Mess Around with Jim." This song told the cautionary tale of a man thought to be physically unbeatable by those who knew of him, his persona being that of a barroom brawler of the first degree! He was roundly thought to be invincible, until he met a man named Slim. Up until that time, those who had thoughts of contesting Jim retreated, knowing that there would be dire consequences for them if they did.

The simple message from these words is that if you decide to take on an established and well-recognized power, you will pay a price. The same message is well understood in the educational establishment, within the ranks of the education coterie. If you proffer an alternative viewpoint about something deemed to be "settled science" in the eyes of those in power, you will pay! Principals, on the front lines in the public schools, know this risk well. They know that they will be at high risk should they depart from the *party line* regarding teacher evaluation—that to which everyone in the coterie purports to subscribe.

Consider for a moment the "price" a high school principal would pay were he/she to challenge the appropriateness of referencing a student with the "wrong pronoun." As has been seen by the uniformly conformed positions schools mandate on the matter of transgenderism, this principal would be in deep trouble. Risky business, going outside the lines of coterie-conformed thinking! And as has been seen, the education coterie is in a virtual lockstep when it comes to matters involving the delicate issue of transgenderism.

Were a school principal to reference a male student by *his* male name, if the male student wanted to be referred to as a female, it would be a nearly unforgivable violation of group-think norms, especially were the assertion of the wrong name to be repeated over time. "Bigot," "homophobe," "misogynist," or "genderphobe" are but a few of the labels some would affix to the person found guilty of "misgendering" this student. Notwithstanding that none of these terms legitimately describes the principal's behavior, they could be the kiss of death for the principal's career in the school district wherein this "infraction" occurred. As has been said, the coterie's influence is both pervasive and strong!

The consequences for asserting an unpopular idea, be it about transgenderism or teacher evaluation, is what keeps most school officials from voicing what they likely know are some *academically honest* ways of dealing with issues. As has been demonstrated in the case of transgenderism, there is a wealth of scientific and social research that speaks against reinforcing young people's beliefs, particularly at young ages, that they are a sex other than that of their birth. Similarly, it has been shown that current teacher evaluation systems are seriously flawed, to the extent that they are rendered largely useless in addressing measures of teaching performance quality.

Local boards of education, superintendents, and building principals have maintained systems of teacher evaluation for decades that appear very much like the emperor sporting his new clothes. Everyone knows that the systems are empirically and academically naked, but no one risks making a strong argument that they are. Why take the risk of alienating not only local officials, but also well-respected state and national organizations such as those referenced earlier? "Why kick a hornet's nest?" might be the thinking of those who see dysfunctionality but are reluctant to address it. In such a circumstance, it's not unusual that *keeping* one's job takes on a higher priority than *doing* one's job.

In the interest of not labeling any person or persons as responsible for the current circumstance, as many people coalesce to keep it alive, the matter at hand is resolvable by the animation of one human trait— *courage*. There is no remedy for this existential circumstance other than professional courage, courage to address issues herein defined as public education's 21st-century *third-rail* issues. These are the issues of *political* correctness, not *correctness*. One of these is teacher evaluation.

In the case of teacher evaluation, it is the school principal who, having the greatest insights, speaks out the least. The principal is the person most culpable for failing to address the flawed methods by which teachers are evaluated, because it is the principal who acts in its perpetration. But there are reasons why principals have remained relatively silent about a duty they are contractually required to perform. In the sphere of public education, the school principal is the person with the greatest exposure for admonition, and the fewest protections against the negative consequences that might accrue from such.

In almost all public school districts, the teachers have employment contracts that protect them from being fired by their superiors. Superintendents, while serving at the behest of their boards of education, typically work under the terms of multiyear contracts. Even the custodians and secretarial staff have contracts that protect their job security. Building principals are the *only* ones who have no such protections. They work from year to year with no contractual protections to protect their employment status from one year to the next. Watching their Ps and Qs in matters such as teacher evaluation, matters framed as "the accepted way of things" by everyone with whom they work, can become a compelling motivation!

The matter of "Don't mess around with Jim" because you'll *pay* is not presented here to generate sympathy for principals, or any others in the education coterie. It is presented merely to show that the *leadership* needed to make meaningful changes in education, that leadership previously defined as sorely lacking in school people, is what is needed to change the failed teacher evaluation circumstance that has existed for years. But school leadership, the number-one role of the principal, is unprotected when put into action. Everyone involved in public education, perhaps excepting parents, knows this.

When considering the arguments that will be made in the following pages for how teacher evaluation systems can be made better, keep in mind that the "Don't mess around with Jim" caution will *always* be in the minds of those who *could* lead—lead to a better circumstance for everyone. This is an important frame through which the solutions to be presented should be viewed by those considering whether or not they could, in reality, become implemented in today's public schools. Once again, this is not cited as an excuse. It is merely an existentially objective reality.

PRINCIPALS' CONTENT-KNOWLEDGE INEPTITUDE: KNOWING, AND *ACKNOWLEDGING*, THAT YOU KNOW YOU DON'T KNOW!

Perhaps the most serious flaw to current teacher evaluation protocols is that principals are not competent to judge whether or not their teachers are teaching true and accurate content. And as has been said earlier, most principals, if honest, will admit that they know little to nothing about the subject areas their teachers teach. However, they are still required by their immediate supervisors to perform evaluations about the teaching of these subjects. It is a dilemma that has bedeviled principals since the responsibility for teacher evaluation was added to their job descriptions.

"There is no substitute for accurate knowledge. Know yourself, *know your business*, know your men."[3] These are the words of car-guy Lee Iacocca. Iacocca is the man who spearheaded the development of the Mustang and Pinto when he was with the Ford Motor Company in the 1960s, and then brought Chrysler Corporation back from the brink of bankruptcy in the 1980s. A no-nonsense kind of leader, Iacocca knew what he knew, and also knew what he *didn't* know. And when he didn't know something, he found people who *did* know.

Perhaps the most important advice Iacocca offered in his statement is about the need to "know yourself." It is this primary criterion for leadership that principals seem to have failed to come to grips with, at least insofar as it relates to their teacher evaluation duties. Principals do not seem either able or willing to address the existential fact that they do not *know* the subject content, that taught by their teachers, to be able to evaluate their teachers in their teaching of the content. They do not appear to recognize the limitation their content ignorance bestows upon them. The dialogue line from a Clint Eastwood film, *Magnum Force*, is apropos: "A man's got to know his limitations."[4] Apparently, principals do not.

Principals need to know, and acknowledge, that they are severely limited by their lack of subject-matter knowledge when evaluating their teachers. But there is a way to both recognize the limitation and deal with it effectively. Do what Lee Iacocca did. Go out and find people who know what you don't know! Once found, these people can be enjoined to compensate for principals' deficits in the areas wherein they have limited or no knowledge—subjects such as chemistry, biology, French, history, trigonometry, etc.

Good leaders, like Lee Iacocca, know that they don't know everything they need to know to do their jobs and that they might not find those who *do* know inside their own organizations. The *province* Lee Iacocca worked within was one major automobile company, but he was not *provincial* in his leadership style. Iacocca was willing to go outside his own backyard to find the right people, those who could fill in his own deficits in knowledge. This is precisely what school principals need to do to resolve their subject knowledge deficiencies. They need to get out of their own backyards!

A PARADIGM SHIFT IN TEACHER EVALUATION: FINDING THOSE WHO *DO* KNOW TO SUBSTITUTE FOR THOSE WHO *DON'T* KNOW

As the late Dr. Kenneth McFarland stated, "There's no substitute for knowing!"[5] But not knowing is not a fatal condition. As stated, the condition can be remedied quite easily by finding someone who knows! This is what is needed for principals to resolve their deficiencies of subject-matter knowledge. They simply need to find people who possess the subject-matter knowledge that they do not, and then engage them in evaluating teachers in their respective areas of expertise. And these are both abundant and available! They are, as of today, an untapped resource, one that can be a real *value-added* resource pool for public education.

Just as Lee Iacocca found people qualified to watch over the building of his automobiles, those with expertise in various aspects of automotive design and assembly, school principals can find qualified people to evaluate the subject-matter competencies of their teachers. Subject-matter experts are available for *every* subject taught in the public schools today, and they are to be found in abundance in workplace America today.

CONTENT EXPERTISE: SOME EXAMPLES OF WHERE TO FIND IT

America, the most successful capitalist country in the world, affords educators a virtually unlimited number of workplace venues in which content expertise may be found. From the narrowly academic fields of science, the domains of business and industry, and myriad others, content acumen is available for application in the public schools. Some examples will display this.

People with expertise in chemistry can be found working in research and development at companies such as Dow Chemical and LyondellBasell Industries. These two rank number one and number two among the top ten such companies in the United States.[6] As such, they employ hundreds of chemists, each adding their unique chemistry skill sets to their companies' marketplace success.

One of the most difficult areas of subject-matter knowledge for principals is the field of foreign languages. Most speak no other language than English. But all major universities have departments dedicated to the study of foreign language, almost any language found on the globe today. As teachers at these institutions are deemed experts in their subject areas, why not engage them in evaluating those who teach the languages they teach: public school foreign language teachers?

Similar to foreign languages, universities employ professors in *all* fields of academic teaching and research. All of these could be tapped, for their expertise, for every subject currently taught in the public schools. And where other sources might be added into the mix, business, industry, and other workplace venues active in the American economy today would be able to offer experts in every field of work imaginable.

All the expertise needed, that which is currently lacking for the evaluation of subject-matter competence in schools today, is found in everyday working America! If the schools could, somehow, gain access to the abundance of experts currently working in the community workplaces, those that keep the American economy functioning, the oft-cited value of *diversity* might be accomplished in a truly *meaningful* way, not merely as a meaningless shibboleth asserted by the coterie.

PEDAGOGICAL EXPERTISE: SOME EXAMPLES OF WHERE TO FIND IT

Just as universities can be repositories of subject-matter expertise, so too can they be repositories for pedagogical skill sets. Colleges of education, the very *best* ones, have highly respected educators engaged in training prospective teachers. These professors of pedagogical excellence could be accessed for their knowledge in evaluating the teaching skills of teachers in the public schools. In addition to colleges of education, other university colleges, such as business and communications, are repositories of skill sets that are highly related to teaching performance in the public schools. More about this later.

In addition to college professors of education, organizations such as Relay/GSE[7] and Sposato School of Education[8] are resources that could be accessed for this same purpose. Even commercial ventures such as

Sylvan Learning Centers[9] can be tapped for the expertise their instructors and staff have to offer. These, and others, can provide public school principals with levels of expertise in evaluating teachers' pedagogical skills that, at a minimum, go well beyond the knowledge and experiences of principals.

While it will take a bit of a leap of faith for public school employees to seek the counsel of those outside their own *neighborhoods*, those over which they currently reign, such an outreach, if sought, would provide them a far better assessment of the pedagogical abilities of their teachers. Asking for assistance from the public, for-profit sector will undoubtedly cause some to experience some feelings of inadequacy. But that's the point! Principals are *not adequate*, up to the task of evaluating their teachers, at least without some informed assistance.

The ability of principals to *know their limitations* becomes paramount in resolving the teacher evaluation deficiencies in the public schools today. If egos, either individual or organizational, live so large so as to preclude requesting and receiving good counsel from outside the schools, the programs advocated herein will be rejected out of hand. All of what is offered here is predicated upon the high degree of professionalism so often discussed among public school people, and promoted to their constituents. The kind of venture suggested by this approach will put the professionalism of educators, both teachers and principals, to the test.

CONTENT AND PEDAGOGICAL EXPERTISE: A FINAL WORD

School principals are not qualified to evaluate either the subject content or pedagogy of teaching performances, those they would witness by observing their teachers in their classrooms. And notwithstanding the special trainings they might receive prior to the beginning of school years, these are merely stopgap measures intended to shore up their recognized inadequacies in knowledge and skills. Principals would need to know more, and their teachers should expect more, if high-quality teacher evaluation is the result to which they collectively aspire.

The deficits in both content and pedagogical knowledge, those experienced by today's public school principals, is simply a *bridge too far*, precluding achievement of the quality teacher evaluation that is desired. And as yet another report card for educational reform suggests, much of what is currently promoted as good teaching practice, by principals, is misguided.

In 2014, Rob Coe of Durham University, in England, noted

in a report on what makes great teaching that many commonly used classroom techniques do not work. Unearned praise, grouping by ability, and accepting or encouraging children's different "learning styles" are widely espoused but bad ideas. So too is the notion that pupils can discover complex ideas all by themselves. Teachers must *impart knowledge* and critical thinking.

Those who do embody six aspects of great teaching, as identified by Mr. Coe. The first and second concern their motives and how they get on with their peers. The third and fourth involve using time well, fostering good behavior and high expectations. Most important, though, are the fifth and sixth aspects, high-quality instruction and so-called "pedagogical content knowledge"—*a blend of subject knowledge and teaching craft*. Its essence is defined by Charles Chew, one of Singapore's "principal master teachers," an elite group that guides the island's schools: "I don't teach physics; I teach my pupils how to learn physics."[10] (emphasis mine)

Once again, content (subject-matter strength) and the ability to present it (strong pedagogical expertise) are reported to be the two *most* important parts of a good teaching performance. *Both* must be addressed if teaching performances are to be assessed with a proper degree of efficacy. And if they are to be so addressed, principals will need some new methodologies they have heretofore not had in their possession.

USING NEW TOOLS TO SOLVE OLD PROBLEMS: TECHNOLOGY TO THE RESCUE!

In 1990, Garrison Keillor spun one of his tales about his mythical hometown, Lake Wobegon. In his radio monologue that evening, Keillor told a story he titled "A Day in the Life of Clarence Bunsen." In this story, Keillor recounted the experience of an aging man who took the opportunity to relive some of the things he liked to do when he was a child. As he saw some young boys approaching through a deeply wooded area, he climbed up into the branches of a tree and watched as they, unaware of his presence up there, came wandering by.

Keillor told of how Clarence liked to *watch* people. Clarence enjoyed watching them doing whatever they were doing—but to do so in secrecy. Now, perched up in a tree, he watched as these young boys came trooping by. Keillor recounted Clarence's thoughts:

> And it wasn't as though he wanted to see anything embarrassing or shameful. He said that he just liked to look at people when they thought that they weren't being watched. People are different when they don't know you're looking at 'em. They act more natural you know, like animals; like these kids down there, leaning forward, bodies all wired up, listening so hard you could almost hear 'em listen.[11]

It's like that in teacher evaluation! It *should* be like sitting in a tree to see what you might not see if those you were watching knew you were watching them! But when the principal sits in a classroom to watch, both the kids *and* the teacher act differently. They act differently than they would if no one was watching, just like in Keillor's story. So does everyone in public education, teachers, principals, superintendents, and others, fail to understand what Keillor explained so well in his story? If they do, then why do they keep doing it?!

Keillor's carefully crafted words in telling his story ring so vibrant and true because he is describing a common-sense activity, one easily understood by everyone in his audience listening to it. Everyone gets it! They cannot escape the simple wisdom presented to them so humbly by this storyteller. But how is it that principals, and others associated with teacher evaluations, *don't* get it?!

In any classroom, when the principal comes in and sits down at the rear of the room, the older students likely know that their teacher is being evaluated. Younger children may not. But whatever the ages, is it not obvious that the principal's presence alters how the students behave? Even in cases where teachers alert their students that the principal is coming to class the next day, as many will do, the mindsets of the students, and possibly also their behaviors, cannot help but be changed by this change in classroom protocol.

Regardless of age, experienced principals know that an administrative presence will *always* change the classroom atmosphere, and sometimes for the worse. A *difficult* student might seize the opportunity to test the teacher, doing something provocative just to see what action it might elicit from the teacher in the presence of *the boss*. Most will likely try to maintain a sense of normalcy while knowing that their teacher is being scrutinized, but their volitional intent, in and of itself, changes their behavior. And the teachers, particularly those newer to their duties, also act differently than they would if not for being watched. Being watched just changes people, in this case students *and* teachers.

What if principals could evaluate the performance of their teachers without entering *physically* into the process at all? What if teachers could be observed by the principal while teaching their classes but have no principal in the classroom while they are teaching their classes?

A "WHAT IF?": OBSERVING IN ABSENTIA

What if the principal could watch a teacher teach a class without having to sit in the classroom watching it happen? Wouldn't any teaching performance be more normal if the students and teacher were the only ones in the classroom, as is normally the situation?

Whenever a principal enters a classroom, his/her presence alters the learning atmosphere for both the teacher and the students, regardless of who or what the principal represents to either. It's just a boots-on-the-ground reality! So if this were changed, wouldn't the situation change for the better?

In order to eliminate the intrusive presence of principals sitting at the back of classrooms watching teachers as they teach, some fairly simple yet state-of-the-art technology can be brought to bear. Simply stated, a video-recording camera could be unobtrusively located at the rear of the classroom. In a fixed position and providing a complete wide-angle view of the classroom, this camera could be activated by the teacher, with no notice taken by the students.

In this scenario, not only the principal would be absent from the classroom, but he/she would have no control over when a teacher's performance would be subject to observation. The teacher has unilateral control of when the camera is turned on and off. With this sole control, the teacher chooses which class or classes are to be recorded, and also which of these are to be submitted to the principal for review.

As was described earlier, students come to their classes each day with different conditions affecting their lives on those days, their personal baggage. They are tired or alert, focused or distracted, physically strong or weak, healthy or feeling pain and discomfort. Teachers are the same. They too come to their classes with their own personal baggage. This being the case, it is highly appropriate to allow teachers to select the days when they are feeling their very best, confident that they will be performing their teaching activities at the top of their games.

Over an agreed-upon period of time, perhaps semesters of grading periods, teachers would be required to provide the principal with a specified number of classroom teaching performances by a predetermined date, perhaps three or four. Again, the teacher decides not only which classes are recorded, but also which of these are submitted to the principal. Teachers may choose to record several teaching performances and then select out those they believe are their best, those to be submitted to the principal. This allows the teachers to select their very best performances.

With teachers having the latitude to determine their best teaching performances, they can be sure that what their principals see are the best they have to offer. From another perspective, principals know that what they are seeing represents a best-case scenario as well. Knowing that a person's good days typically outnumber their bad days, choosing to see only the good ones is appropriate for both teacher and principal.

However, if principals would like to play a more active role in determining what they will be seeing, they might direct teachers to record a class, one that the principal wishes to see. In this scenario, the principal would inform the teacher, at the beginning of the school day, which class is to be recorded. This principal-selected class will be included with those chosen by the teacher, later to be submitted to the principal. While still weighted toward the teacher's selections, this would allow for a degree of spontaneity to be added into the process.

Note that all of the recording and transmission of recordings can be accomplished electronically, absent the need for any physical articles of transmittal. As such, sending and receiving classroom teaching performance recordings is accomplished with a mere keystroke. And as was mentioned, this format eliminates principals' intrusions into classrooms, hurried note-taking during observations, and an overall improvement in lessening of tensions associated with the observation procedure—for teachers, principals, and students.

THE PRINCIPAL HAS THE RECORDINGS: NOW WHAT?

In possession of the recordings of the teacher's classroom performances, the principal now engages the participation of others, those subject-content and pedagogy resources people previously referenced. The recordings, electronically transmitted to these people, are reviewed. The resource people will then provide an electronically transmitted written narrative review of the teacher's teaching performance to the principal. Included in this narrative will be predetermined performance categories, those defined by teachers, principals, and the outside resource people prior to engaging the process.

The logistical considerations for assembling the cohort groupings required for this process, the subject content and pedagogy resource people, will not be a matter for discussion here. However, suffice it to say that these resource people would become parts of nationally established and maintained registries, one for pedagogy and another for subject content. Through ongoing networking practices, this assemblage of resource people would continue to expand over time, allowing school districts to access both state-specific and national pools of subject content and pedagogy expertise.

Once the principal receives the feedback from the resource people selected for providing it, the principal now has the information needed to compile a comprehensive assessment of the teaching observed. But what role, other than merely compiling the information received, should the principal play? Is the *entire* process outsourced, leaving the principal a mere conveyor of information attained?

The qualifications of principals, those needed to accurately assess their teachers' subject content and pedagogical skills, have been shown to be less than what are required, at least in terms of how they are applied to the teacher evaluation procedure. However, principals know the natures and personalities of their teachers better than any outsiders, those enlisted to evaluate their performances, could know them. And this is a most critically important key in defining the role that principals have in the evaluation of their teachers. It is this: Principals have a unique perspective on who their teachers are as they enter their school buildings each morning. Any evaluation, absent this knowledge, would be unacceptably deficient!

In many school districts, principals have the opportunity to interview candidates for teaching positions that arise in their buildings. Boards of education are legally responsible for hiring teachers for their school districts, but principals are typically afforded the opportunity to recommend those whom they would like the board to hire. Barring unusual circumstances, these are the teachers that are hired. In the interviewing phase, it is likely that principals seek some unique personal characteristics in those they hire, those characteristics that would make them both good teachers and a good fit with the existing teaching staff. And these characteristics vary widely from person to person, none being of a cookie-cutter kind that all possess.

One teacher might have a unique way of utilizing humor, sometimes sarcasm, in his/her practice of teaching. Having this quality, this teacher gains students' attention, keeping them on their toes, the students not knowing when their teacher might *slip one in* on them! Being more or less a natural gift, this teacher uses a strategy that not every teacher could use. And as everyone knows, from thinking back to the teachers who were their favorites when they were in school, *these* are the kinds of things that stand out in memory—the things that make one teacher *very* special in the eyes of students!

Another teacher, also highly regarded by students, those same students who enjoyed the humor of the other just mentioned, would enjoy another teacher for very different reasons. This teacher might be routinely stern and demanding and yet able to convey a deeply sincere caring for students. While perhaps stodgy, unrelenting, and rigid, this teacher's students perceive more than the just an outward demeanor. Mere mannerisms, those that color the words the teacher utters, do not detract from what students hear, and feel, this teacher transmitting to them.

Each teacher, while widely different in who they were and how they taught, engendered a high receptivity for learning in these same students. Neither teacher can, or should, be evaluated based on what one has that the other does not. All being different over a wide range of teaching styles and approaches, teachers arrive at effectiveness through different routes of travel. Again, as was previously noted, a cookie-cutter/one-size-fits-all approach to teacher evaluation is inappropriate. There is no one way, and principals are *uniquely* positioned to recognize teachers for what *they* bring to the practice of teaching their students. To evaluate otherwise does a disservice to everyone involved, teachers, principals, and most certainly students.

Principals, unlike those outside experts they solicit to provide them nuts-and-bolts data, know that the data will be meaningless absent someone effectively translating it to the one in need of receiving it. There's no one better able to finish this final and *most* important step in teacher evaluation than the principal. While the principal solicits the hard data from others, those lacking a *human* knowledge of the teacher, principals have the ability to provide this most important value-added ingredient.

Teacher evaluation is partly about principals, through classroom video observations, arriving at an opinion of teachers' teaching acumen. But that's only *half* the process. The other half has to do with presenting their composite of views to the teachers, and the teachers accepting and integrating what they receive to the benefit of their teaching practices. It is in this presenting/receiving genre that teacher evaluation either succeeds to achieve its purpose, or fails.

The unique positions that principals occupy and the critical roles they can and should play in the evaluation of teachers cannot be overstated. But their efforts must be focused on the proper venues, those wherein the skill sets they possess can be most effectively applied. As has been the practice for decades, principals have allowed themselves to be placed into venues wherein they are ill equipped to perform. If teacher evaluation is to achieve its proper function, this must stop. Principals should be called upon to perform in those venues wherein they are uniquely qualified to perform.

That principals should become sanguine with performing *only* the tasks for which they are qualified is long overdue! Giving over tasks, those they are unqualified to perform, to others is a sign of *true* professionalism. This is an important distinction that needs to be made by those seeking to engage the processes described. Some will suggest that outsourcing *any* portion of the teacher evaluation procedure to others, whomever they might be, is a sign that principals are abandoning their professional responsibilities. But this is the situation viewed upside down! Principals choosing this approach are, in fact, embracing their responsibilities by seeing to it that they are carried out in the most effective manner.

As has been described in the preceding sections, principals have been *routinely* saddled with tasks they have not had the abilities to perform. And the key word is "routinely"! That which virtually *all* public schools have done since teacher evaluations came into being was done *routinely*. With a tweak here, and a tweak there, not much has changed over the past decades in the *routine* of teacher evaluation, with the possible exception that the monotony of the process has been increased for everyone involved!

There is no weighting in one area of performance that is better, of more value, than another. Of what value is content knowledge if it cannot be conveyed effectively to another? A teacher highly proficient in knowledge of biology is a failure if that knowledge cannot be effectively transmitted to students. Conversely, the best transmitter, absent content knowledge, transmits nothing of value. Good teaching is defined by the presence of both, and a good evaluation of that teaching must include the assessment of both.

A principal's evaluation of a teaching performance relies upon the principal's competence to ascertain information about the teacher being evaluated in three areas: content knowledge, pedagogical knowledge, and communication skills. In the first two, content and pedagogy, principals are informed via the outside sources previously referenced. However, in the area of communication skills, principals must be informed by their own knowledge of effective communication. In a word, principals *must* have excellent communication skills themselves in order to be able to evaluate this trait in their teachers. Each of these skill sets is unique, requiring the evaluator to have, or to be able to ascertain, a high degree of competence.

The combination of these three coalesce in a cohesive evaluation of a teaching performance. All three are required as they apply to teacher evaluation, and yet each is a unique *cognitive* knowledge category. As was described earlier, principals are frequently not experts in all three. This is why principals should *farm out* the unique areas of content and pedagogy to those competent to assess them, while retaining the area of communication to themselves. It is assumed, hopefully correctly, that principals are effective communicators themselves, thereby competent to adjudicate the effectiveness of their teachers.

The *human* aspects of teaching, those personally associated intangibles that every teacher brings to his or her students every day, cannot be overemphasized. The personal traits that a Jaime Escalante brings, while not like any other teacher, are what must be factored into the mix in teacher evaluation. Along with content competency and the excellent communication skills that result in delivery proficiency, these *human elements* are the things that complete the circuit in teaching proficiency. Principals are in a unique position to see how these impact the totality of a teacher's performance. *Outsiders*, whatever other qualifications they may bring to the table, cannot know these as does the teacher's principal.

THE FINAL STEP: BRINGING INFORMATION TO BEAR

The data having been obtained in the areas of content and pedagogy, principals are now in possession of the information they need to hold a meaningful get-together with the teacher whose performance is being reviewed. As the *outside* reviewers of the teaching performances have done, the principal can now utilize the same recordings in choreographing a conference with the teacher. Both teacher and principal can now sit together, reviewing and discussing portions of video recordings. The interactivity between principal and teacher, which allows for pinpoint targeting of things seen that are of issue, is now facilitated through both parties seeing the same things at the same time.

The recordings afford the principal the opportunity to point out real-time teaching behaviors that both can see in the video recordings. The teacher, simultaneously witnessing what the principal is pointing out, can address each with specificity. The principal now has no use for hastily written notes while observing a classroom teaching presentation, those jotted down while simultaneously trying to remain attentive to what was being said by the teacher. And the teacher need not struggle to remember what the principal is referencing—that which the principal recorded, in hastily written notes, while observing a classroom teaching performance.

The *rest of the story* now becomes about teachers being empowered, newly equipped with authoritative and respected insights regarding the performance of their craft. Now, knowing that the practice of their teaching has been reviewed by those well qualified to do so, teachers can be confident that they are being provided substantively sound guidance. This is the scenario in play as senior physicians evaluate the performances of their interns.

Some might believe that the *intern–senior physician* paradigm might be acceptable for *new* teachers, those lacking some years of experience, but that experienced teachers would have reason to reject the intern–senior physician characterization. But the analogy of the *practice* of medicine to the *practice* of teaching is applicable for all engaged in the practice of teaching. Both teach *art forms*. As such, neither achieves what could be termed a *settled status*, static and unchanging over time. Both, if they are to remain innovative and self-improving over time, must avail themselves to ongoing evaluation and refinement of their respective practices.

Senior physicians routinely stay current with medical journals, those that treat with the medical specialties of their practices, and they engage with state-of-the-art training in new developments and protocols in their areas of specialization. No physician, regardless of the field of specialization (obstetrics, orthopedics, neurology, etc.) can afford to practice over time while relying solely on his/her initial medical school training.

Similarly, no teacher, regardless of the field of specialization (biology, mathematics, history, etc.) can afford to do any differently. A biology teacher, for example, will remain current via reading appropriate journals and articles relating to his/her realm of academic study. So too should these teachers engage state-of-the-art training in their chosen field. Both professions call for ongoing learning and the improvement of skill sets. None can be *top gun* absent this ongoing commitment to improvement.

THE PERCEPTION OF TEACHERS' STATUS: WHY HAS IT CHANGED?

In recent years, the US public has come to view teachers in a manner very dissimilar to the way publics in other countries view their teachers. In Japan for example, the citizenry has high regard for those who teach in the public schools. And the salaries paid them, somewhat higher than what is paid in the United States, provide only a subtle reflection of this. Does salary alone provide a realistic picture of the status of teachers in Japan, the United States, or any country for that matter? Perhaps more far-reaching than the effect of salary, cultural differences likely play a much larger role in the way teachers are perceived.

Japan, as a country whose students routinely outperform those in the United States in testing achievement scores, may have something to teach public school educators in the United States. And it is this: It's about *decorum*! Decorum in Japan's schools relates not only to how people *treat* each other, how students treat their teachers and vice versa, but how they *appear* to each other. Yes, how students, and teachers, *look* during the school day does make a difference!

In Japan, both students and teachers adhere to a dress code, one that would be seen as "radical" in today's American schools. Nearly all secondary school students are required to wear uniforms. The traditional uniform is a high-collared, black, military-style suit for boys and a beribboned sailor blouse and pleated skirt for girls (sorry, ladies, there's no pants option). Besides regulating clothing, shoes, and backpacks, many Japanese secondary schools impose strict bans on makeup, nail polish, hairstyles, and even eyebrow grooming that would make the average American teen wince.[12]

This kind of outwardly expressed decorum, the clothing people wear, bespeaks a larger issue in Japanese schools, that of the behavior of the students. As is typical in Japan's secondary schools when a teacher calls in sick, the school does not call in a substitute: "instead, students are trusted to study quietly and independently."[13] And the same degree of self-control and respect for the educational *process* is reflected in the manner in which students treat their teachers: "At the beginning and end of each class, students stand and greet the teacher, then bow in unison."[14]

It is highly unlikely that people in this country would think that their child should stand and bow to a teacher, and most would not tolerate their child's *expression of self* to be infringed by makeup, hairstyle, or any other form of "restrictive rulings" made by their schools. And teachers mirror this same sentiment. A visit to almost any public school in the United States will show some teachers to be dressing poorly, not at all in keeping with the "professional" status they claim.

Many teachers in today's American schools dress in ways that closely resemble their students. Many teachers, both men and women, routinely *dress down* in wearing attire that would likely not differentiate teacher from student. Jeans, in some cases sporting "stylish" holes, sneakers, and other such are commonly worn by teachers in public schools today. But not in Japan! For both men and women teaching in Japan, their manner of dress displays a higher degree of decorum:

Men

- Top: A collared shirt is best. Sometimes polo shirts are okay, but usually you'll be wearing a button down shirt. If a tie fits in the collar, then it's probably a good choice.
- Bottom: Slacks or khakis are standard. But dark colored slacks are better. No jeans, shorts, or sweatpants.

Women

- Top: Blouses or sweaters are good choices. Sleeveless shirts are generally not appropriate unless covered by a cardigan. Short sleeve blouses shouldn't be too short.
- Bottom: Bottoms should be slacks, but not jeans, leggings, or sweatpants. Skirts are fine as long as they are below the knee and don't hug the body too much.[15]

Once again, it should be noted that Japan's culture largely circumscribes that which is permitted in Japanese schools, just as American culture does in America. But that's a very big difference! One culture maintains a pattern of decorous behavior for both students and teachers, while another does not. American teachers, dressing, speaking, and in some cases even acting as their students do, should not expect their students to see them as different from themselves, the students.

As they should, most parents ascribe a higher level of maturity to their children's teachers than they do to their children. Accruing not only to the relative differences in age that separate most teachers from the students they teach, parents tend to respect the university degrees their children's teachers have achieved, oftentimes a higher status than their own. Often owing to these differences, parents expect their children's teachers to behave differently than their children in keeping with their expectations.

However, seeing teachers behave in ways that mirror their children's behaviors raises parents' concern that they may have been incorrect in their ascription of *higher-order* behavior. With increasing frequency, parents hear the language spoken by their children's teachers to be largely the *same* as their children's. They hear the word "like" employed as a prefix to words when no comparison motif is intended. (Example: "She was, *like*, going to tell him to go away!") In a similar fashion, parents are not incorrect in wondering why teachers tend to describe *so* many things as "awesome," as do the sophomoric students they teach. There's more, but these all-too-common examples suffice to make the point.

The professional status that many teachers claim they are due, but do not receive, is increasingly seen by parents as a cause-and-effect situation. In a word, parents have increasingly begun to adopt an "If they want respect, they should act differently!" point of view. This view is not helped any by the increasing frequency of news stories, both national and local, that continue to appear in the local and national media. Stories of teachers behaving badly in their classrooms are not helping them maintain their status as "professionals."

An increasing number of stories wherein teachers have been seen acting badly are creating a harmful schism between parents and teachers. Stories that show teachers reaching well beyond what most parents would deem reasonable create a "them and us" separation that, in the long term, is damaging to the education of students. As was discussed in chapter 2, teachers in Badger Middle School decided to teach content that was beyond the board-approved curriculum, the "white privilege" issue, and parents rose up and complained. [16]

The Badger Middle School scenario is but one of many such stories that hit the national media today. Stories like these, heretofore seen as isolated incidences, have become increasingly common in media reporting. Some people see this as a natural, while unintended, consequence of their schools becoming less and less formal in the ways they carry out their educational functions. The "do your own thing" era prevalent in the 1960s may have faded into history, but some of the mindsets of that era have not. Many major universities in America today find themselves populated by those who advocated radical agendas in the '60s. Some of the same can be found in the public schools as well, now advocating the heretofore referenced "social justice" issues that are their causes today.

This is another reason for principals to become much more *meaningfully* engaged in evaluating their teachers in ways that they've not needed to be involved in the past. In today's schools, where some teachers see their roles as social justice advocates in addition to teaching the classes assigned them, principals must be increasingly watchful. It is this venue of need that makes it imperative that principals carefully scrutinize their teachers' classroom performances, via those recorded sessions sent to the outside resources previously referenced.

WHAT FLIES UNDER THE RADAR, REVISITED: THE OVERREACH OF SOME TEACHERS

The matter of teachers teaching beyond the approved curriculum can occur via two different routes. Some teachers may inject material into their lessons that is not included in the board-approved curriculum. The Wisconsin middle school teachers teaching "white privilege" is an example of this. Others, while teaching within the approved curriculum, choose to teach their *bias* about a subject. In so doing, they teach topics in a one-sided manner, neglecting salient information that could tend to distract from their personal opinions. What makes this circumstance difficult for principals is that others in their profession may actually sanction this behavior, those in the heretofore referenced education coterie.

Oftentimes, but not exclusively, these forms of teacher malpractice can easily find entry into the science curriculum of public schools. "Climate change" provides an object example wherein a coterie member, the ASCD (Association for Supervision and Curriculum Development), advocates for *one-sided* teaching. The May 2017 issue of its *Education*

Update publication contains an article titled "When Teaching Climate Change, Knowledge Is Power." Sounds like a reasonable article—until it is read!

This article advocates the oft-cited claim that climate change is "settled science," and it further states that this view is based upon the power of "knowledge." But knowledge, at least *complete knowledge*, would entail the recognition that this article presents but one side of this issue. The article fails to cite information, soundly arrived-at data, that argues against the claims that climate change is a matter that has been settled via science. A few selected passages will show the bias resident in this article.

The article describes a parent, who at a meeting with his child's science teacher and school principal, says to both, "There's no scientific consensus on this. . . . Why aren't you teaching both sides?"[17] The article then postulates, "This is the kind of moment that every educator who teaches climate change dreads."[18] In reading this, two questions could be asked of the writer of this article. First, why does the article begin by referencing the topic with biased terminology, "climate *change*," when "climate science" would be a bias-free reference? Also, why would any teacher of this subject *dread* a parent asking questions?

Further reading of the article further displays the ASCD's bias about this subject, which results in its advocating that teachers teach in a one-sided manner. The article references the National Center for Science Education. The ASCD, and the National Center for Science Education it cites, both suggest that those who might disagree with its position (that advanced by the ASCD in the article) are to be politely *tolerated*, but not engaged in discussion. Both the ASCD and the NCSE appear to believe that those students who disagree are merely "deniers." The article makes a suggestion for teachers when confronted by these kinds of students:

> The experts at NCSE suggest that teachers confronted with climate change denial in the classroom keep the tone respectful and remember that the student is likely echoing a parent or other trusted adult. However, they warn teachers not to get sucked into an unproductive debate.[19]

A debate engaged by teachers in such a situation, labeled in this article as "unproductive," would likely exclude the data obtained by the

Global Warming Petition Project. This petition, signed by 31,487 American scientists, including 9,029 PhDs, states:

> We urge the United States government to reject the global warming agreement that was written in Kyoto, Japan in December, 1997, and any other similar proposals. The proposed limits on greenhouse gases would harm the environment, hinder the advance of science and technology, and damage the health and welfare of mankind.
>
> There is no convincing scientific evidence that human release of carbon dioxide, methane, or other greenhouse gases is causing or will, in the foreseeable future, cause catastrophic heating of the earth's atmosphere and disruption of the earth's climate. Moreover, there is substantial scientific evidence that increases in atmospheric carbon dioxide produce many beneficial effects upon natural plant and animal environments of the earth.[20]

Could it be that this is the kind of information that, if presented by a student to a teacher, might result in what was referenced as that "unproductive debate," the one that the ASCD cautions teachers should avoid and that science teachers routinely "dread"? Whatever this kind of information *could* be, when it is excluded from the classroom the result is one-sided advocacy-teaching, not knowledge-based teaching.

Such teaching is not, as promoted by the ASCD, that which is predicated on the power of knowledge, but merely *partial* knowledge. The *power of knowledge*, in teaching any subject, must accrue to the presentation of *all* aspects of knowledge, not the selective exclusion of that which does not conform to preassumed bias. Teachers should strive to incorporate the highest degree of content knowledge of the subjects they teach, not select out only the portions of knowledge that conform to their biases. Principals must be on guard for this second kind of teaching in their schools, and prepared to address it in the teacher evaluation processes they employ.

There are more examples of the teaching of one-sided bias, ones that principals may witness being engaged by their teachers. Certainly the LGBT's activist agenda regarding its promotion of transgenderism, that which was presented in chapter 2, is another such example of the one-sided teaching often present in today's public schools. These represent the kinds of *red-flag* issues that principals must expect to encounter in some classrooms.

While principals run the serious risk of offending the devotees of *political correctness*, the issue of *correct teaching* should guide their actions. As mentioned earlier, today's school principals will confront the "Don't Mess Around with Jim" paradigm in evaluating teaching performances, particularly in areas where "Jim" is political correctness incarnate! Those principals who choose to *call the question* on such teaching will be tested, not only by their teachers but likely also by their superiors. In these situations, the most important protocol for principals is, remain steadfast in the requirement that only *truthful* and *accurate* subject content be taught. To accept other constitutes principal malpractice!

TEACHING BIAS IN PLACE OF FACT: THE ROLE OF THE UNIVERSITIES

For those who might think that the matter of teacher bias is overemphasized here, that there is really no cause for alarm and that this phenomenon occurs only rarely in public schools, a final word may help. The word has to with the *cultural* changes that have been taking place in our institutions of higher education. Perhaps dating back to the formation of the SDS (Students for a Democratic Society)[21] in the early 1960s, the focus of university teaching has changed dramatically. The 1960s ushered in an era of student, and teacher, activism, one that pervades American culture today.

The formation of the SDS, and its disruptions to the normal function of society, forever changed the nature of public schooling in America. The tactics advocated by the SDS in the 1960s advocated student protest and institutional disruption, and they have endured to this day. While typically not as violent as the SDS, or its Weather Underground offshoot[22] of the '60s, those who disrupt public schools today engage many of the same tactics these groups used. In public schools, the disruption of order is the goal.

Some students across the country decide that they will not speak in school on the day predetermined by GLSEN (Gay Lesbian Straight Education Network).[23] Students take a vow of silence "to highlight the silencing and erasure of LGBT people at school," according to GLSEN.[24]

As they plan their next school walkout, some students at Marjory Stoneman Douglas High School actively engaged the disruption of their own educations. One student says, "I feel so inspired right now." Another says, "It just shows how many people feel moved to do something."[25] Working with a Black Lives Matter activist, a middle school teacher in Portland, Oregon, is placed on leave after organizing a walkout of students at his school.[26] These are but a few examples of the tactics used to influence public schools today, those that intend to disrupt the normal educational process.

What all of these activities show is that *teachers* are, either actively or passively, involved in the disruption of the educational order at the schools wherein they teach. These "extracurricular" activities also show that schools' leadership does not appear able to control the inappropriate behavior of their students, or teachers. Providing a safe and uninterrupted educational experience and teaching truthful/factually based information are both under attack in the public schools today. Do school principals have the authority they need to take the actions necessary to quell these disturbances to the educational process? If they do, why then are such allowed to continue?

The activities engaged by students, sometimes enabled by their teachers, have their origins in the universities, those that train the teachers. And the universities, as previously referenced, have changed dramatically in recent years. The College of Education at the University of Massachusetts offers a master's degree in "Social Justice Education Concentration."[27] A minimum of four of the following classes are required for the attainment of this degree: "Classism, Heterosexism, Racism, Transgender Oppression and Youth Oppression, Ableism."[28]

When reading these course requirements, recall what the 1983 report, *A Nation at Risk*, said about university teacher preparation programs. The report stated that approximately 41 percent of the classes teachers were required to take were "education courses," not subject-matter courses.[29] As a result, those students graduating from universities, those to become teachers in the public schools, were woefully unprepared in the subjects they would be teaching. The addition of "classism," "ableism," and others of this genre to teacher-training programs does little to improve on the deficiencies the *Nation At Risk* report unearthed so long ago.

Add to this mix the increasingly prominent departments of *gender studies* found on college campuses. Many students studying to become teachers, especially those with a *social justice* orientation, likely enroll in many of the courses offered by these departments. As a result, they find themselves sitting in university classes with the following titles: "bodies," "masculinities," "sex work," "Chicana Lesbian Literature," "LGBTS Issues in Education and Law," "Queering American History," and/or "Contested Sexualities."[30] One might wonder, and legitimately so, how these kinds of subjects might help teachers teach their subject material.

With the knowledge gained in these kinds of courses, as well as many other non-content "education" courses they are required to take, these future teachers graduate with their teaching degrees, ready to teach students in the public schools. And what some teachers will be teaching is other than what most parents think their children will be learning as they send them off to school each morning. The activist-oriented agendas that many new teachers bring to school, those that are incorporated into their teaching, are what make public schooling vastly different than it was in the not-too-distant past. But some universities have also moved to prevent such from entering their classrooms.

To address this phenomenon, some universities have taken steps to retain the character of their institutions by enacting standards of instruction for their teaching staff. For example, Penn State University's policy manual clarifies professional speech, that which is deemed appropriate for the teaching faculty: The faculty member is entitled to freedom in the classroom in discussing his/her subject. The faculty member is, however, responsible for the maintenance of appropriate standards of scholarship and teaching ability. It is not the function of a faculty member in a democracy to indoctrinate his/her students with ready-made conclusions on controversial subjects. The faculty member is expected to train students to think for themselves, and to provide them access to those materials which they need if they are to think intelligently. Hence, in giving instruction upon controversial matters the faculty member is expected to be of a fair and judicial mind, and to set forth justly without super-cession or innuendo, the *divergent opinions of other investigators*.[31] (emphasis mine) If you compare Penn State's standards for teachers with those advocated by the ASCD, those put forth in its clearly activist-oriented *climate change* article, you will see a dramatic difference in what each considers good teaching practice. Most students will not likely be in the classroom of a teacher subscribing to the standards of Penn State University. Students in the public schools will more likely be influenced by the guidelines advocated by the Association for Supervision and Curriculum Development, those advocating the one-sided teaching previously referenced.

What parents whose children attend public schools need to know is that the public schools of today are *not* the public schools they may have attended in their own school days. Furthermore, parents need to recognize that the strength and quality of the principals, those ostensibly leading the public schools, has changed as well.

Managing routine activities such as scheduling, ordering books, or seeing to the building's maintenance, those jobs for which the principal position was created, are no longer the most important parts of being a principal. In 21st-century schooling, seeing to the quality of instruction has risen to be the number-one priority of principals. The changes to the manner in which principals evaluate their teachers' teaching performances, those presented herein, are intended to make principals more effective in keeping with the vastly different challenges they face today.

SOME *NUTS AND BOLTS* CONSIDERATIONS: STRUCTURAL/ORGANIZATIONAL CHANGE

It should be apparent that the kind of *systemic* teacher evaluation change advocated here cannot be implemented in schools absent substantial change. Not only will school principals need to change the ways they perform their daily duties, they will also need retraining to assume some new responsibilities. While this training can be accomplished within school districts, universities will ultimately be called upon to change their training of principals as well. And there will be much more for local districts to do.

School districts around the nation will need to work collaboratively to establish, organize, and maintain a consortium of acknowledged educational *experts* in two areas: (1) Subject-matter expertise: These individuals have high degrees of knowledge in content-specific subjects (biological sciences, languages, political sciences, etc.). They will generate, and provide to the principals, half of the teacher evaluation data;

and (2) Pedagogy specialists: These individuals are highly schooled in expertise in pedagogy, teaching strategies, and presentation techniques. These people will provide the second half of the evaluative data for principals.

Retained for their service in evaluating the contents of the electronic recordings sent to them, the subject-matter and pedagogy specialists will form a nationwide evaluation consortium organized for the purpose of providing principals feedback in their respective areas of expertise: subject-specific content truth/accuracy and pedagogical acumen. Members from each category review recorded teaching performances they receive and then send their findings to the principals who requested their input.

It should be expected that there will be *substantial* logistical considerations relating to how school districts, country-wide, will collaborate in forming and operating this consortium. This is a matter for another discussion, not to be entertained here. Suffice it to say that such an endeavor will call upon public school officials to implement some different ways of doing things, ones for which they will likely need assistance from outside sources. The business community, where production and profit motivate behaviors, should be one of the sources accessed.

Not wishing to add yet another governmental bureaucracy to the mix of those already intruding upon local school districts, engaging a *private* educational entity, such as the Gates Foundation for example, might serve as the coordinating agent in this venture. A strictly *business-oriented* format is needed to gain the best services, and at the best price, for the school districts choosing to participate! And participation should not be mandated, but subject to local boards of education's decisions to engage such a process.

Engaged as a *pilot program*, funding can be obtained through governmental grant sources—local, state, and national. Other funding sources can be sought from professional educational organizations: NASSP (National Association of Secondary School Principals), NAESP (National Association of Elementary School Principals), ASCD (Association for Supervision and Curriculum Development), and others.

The investment in technology, that which is needed for recording classroom teaching, will be significant. More costly will be the reorganization and necessary retraining of administrative staff members: principals, assistant principals, and also those at the central office level. As all will now be performing the teacher evaluation–related tasks differently, new paradigms of performance and accountability will need to be established. While not a subject for consideration herein, the matter of how principals are evaluated is certainly one domain in need of substantial change.

Finally, as the change to teacher evaluation procedures would be dramatic, all those participating must be committed to a process that will take some fine-tuning over time. The logistical components, the installation of cameras and attendant hardware required for classroom observations, can be achieved easily. But the machinations of the people working together, teachers, principals, central office personnel, university and external-venue experts, will be challenging for everyone involved. As in most everything titled "change," success will depend far more on the people than the hardware.

WHAT'S WRONG WITH THIS PICTURE?
THE GOOSE HAS *WAY* TOO MANY LEGS!

Thus far, this story has been about school principals and how they evaluate teachers. As has been shown, it's a *very* big job, one requiring more intellectual capability and skill sets than principals possess. If the limitations cited remain unaltered, and principals continue to perform as they have been shown to be performing, teacher evaluations will continue to lack substance. At worst, they will be a waste of time and effort. But as has also been shown, there are things that can be done, things that change the principal's role to become one that is both workable and effective.

If teacher evaluation were the *only* area wherein the principal's leadership functions were lessened due to a lack of knowledge, an absence of *knowing*, the teacher evaluation "fix" presented here would be enough to resolve the principal's leadership role difficulties. But the principal's leadership role is challenged by many more issues than just an inability to properly evaluate teachers.

The job of being a school principal in today's public schools is simply undoable! It is undoable because the public schools are managed and overseen by people, school superintendents and their local boards of education, who have failed to adjust to societal change. They have failed to recognize that the leadership paradigms of the 19th century are no longer applicable in the 21st century. Specifically, the role of the school principal, as evidenced by the job descriptions for this position, is in need of a substantial overhaul!

REDEFINING THE SCHOOL PRINCIPAL: NEW RESPONSIBILITIES TO MEET NEW NEEDS

As was described earlier, the position of school principal derived from the need to have someone attend to the ever-increasing administrative duties in early schools. Organizing classes, ordering textbooks, seeing to the cleanliness and general order of the school facility, and other such activities were in need of ongoing management. But being an *instructional leader* was not one of these. In today's schools, principals are expected to do all that their predecessors did and also serve as instructional leaders. In today's schools, this is not possible. It's time that the job of the school principal becomes conformed to the reality of 21st-century school leadership needs.

A BRIDGE *TOO* FAR: A JOB *TOO* BIG

As has been stated, the duties principals are expected to accomplish are simply far too extensive for any to be done well. "Pretty good," "As well as can be expected," "Could be better if I had more time," "The best I could with what I had," are all likely descriptors principals would provide, as attainment values, for most of the things they are expected to do each day. But why would these be the responses given by today's principals?

A look at a typical job description, this for a secondary school principal (middle school or high school), shows some of the duties a principal must accomplish:

- Interprets and implements state laws, Board of Education rules, policies, procedures, restructuring and reform efforts, and negotiated contracts.
- Prepares school budgets and is responsible for the monitoring of expenditures of all school funds in accordance with federal, state, and district guidelines.
- Organizes and conducts student extra-curricular activities and fundraising events.
- Participates in directing the school's organization and the appropriate placement of students in accordance with the LAUSD Master Plan for English Learners and as appropriate for desired student outcomes.
- *Ensures the maintenance of a clean physical environment* that is conducive to good health and safety.
- Serves as a resource for and liaison to the stakeholders of the school community.
- Provides guidance, supervision, and assistance in instructional practices and curriculum development that is culturally relevant and responsive to the language, social, and academic needs of all student subgroups, including Standard English Learners, English Learners, Special Education, and gifted and Talented students.
- Evaluates the certified and classified personnel assigned to the school site.
- Performs other duties as assigned.[32]

John Welburn (profiled in a YouTube video)[33] is shown moving about his school while narrating the activities he engages on a typical day as the principal of Hunter High School. Beginning his day at 7:00 a.m., he is seen welcoming students into the school, holding the doors for some as they enter. During the day he is seen in various places in the school, attending a pep assembly in the school gym, meeting with teachers in his office, scrutinizing and reporting a water leak in a hallway, talking with a parent on the telephone, talking with students as they pass between classes in the hallway, monitoring the lunchroom during the lunch period, supervising a football practice session, participating in the pregame preparations for a football game, attending the football game, helping with the cleanup following a football game, and leaving at the end of the day . . . at 10:48 p.m.!

At the end of the video, as Principal Welburn is seen leaving school, he says, "As administrators, our biggest challenge probably is juggling all of those different demands, and yet doing what's best for students."[34] If anything, Principal Welburn's closing statement, "juggling all of those different demands," *vastly* understates the reality of his circumstance! In reality, he knows that a great deal of what he is called upon to do each day goes undone, or not done as well as he'd have liked to do it. All the job responsibilities listed above, those for the Los Angeles Unified School District, are likely much the same as those in his job description.

The truth is, the high school principal's job is *undoable*! The revealing part of all principals' job descriptions, sealing the deal that their jobs are such, is found in the last five words of the Los Angeles job description: "Performs other duties as assigned." While the Los Angeles job description does not list the functions, principals are also responsible for developing, implementing, and monitoring all aspects of students' attendance and discipline in their buildings. In smaller schools, those wherein the principal may have but one assistant if any at all, principals are engaged with student-related issues for a substantial part of every school day. In these schools, circumstantial exigency takes precedence over everything else.

Watching the video with a critical eye reveals that there is no scene showing Mr. Welburn observing a teacher teaching in a classroom, ostensibly the most important part of his job. He is seen talking with a teacher in his office, apparently about that teacher's goals for the school year. But the brevity of this segment in the video portrays a reality of the school principal's role in instructional supervision. The brevity of the scene with the teacher represents the brevity of his role in instructional supervision over the course of the school year.

This brief scene in the video reinforces the *Washington Post* report that principals spend about 12.6 percent of their time "on activities related to instruction."[35] The reality is that most principals spend the *majority* of their time, day after day, in activities that have little or nothing to do with instructional leadership. The current-day activities principals engage, as were those of their predecessors of an earlier time, are most accurately defined as *administrative*, not *educational*.

As was the circumstance when the position of "principal" was created, today's principal is *one person* in charge of supervising and directing *everything* that takes place in the school. But with all the duties principals are expected to perform on a daily basis, instructional supervision, ostensibly the number-one job of principals, is left wanting. With all that arises during the normal course of events in today's public schools, the expectation that instructional improvement will get much attention from the principal is simply *a bridge too far*. And the addition of more and more "assistants" is not the answer. A different design is needed so that the *right* people are in place to do the *right* jobs. It's time that public schools, from the central office to the school buildings, engage in organizational restructuring. Expecting old structures to accommodate new needs is yet another *bridge too far*.

CHANGE IN FORM AND FUNCTION: NEW DESIGNS FOR NEW NEEDS

Like many businesses, public schools are organized in a hierarchical structure. At the top is the principal (tier 1). Below the principal (tier 2) will be assistant principal/s, and below the assistant principal/s will be found all the school staff (tier 3): teachers, teacher aides, guidance counselors, school nurse, secretaries, and maintenance staff. While this structure is acceptable in its current form for the *staff* positions (the third tier), a change in function for the top two *administrative* tiers is needed—for the principal and the assistant principal/s.

As the previously cited job description for the school principal displays, the principal is responsible for *all* building management, including all programs and personnel. But in addition to these responsibilities, the principal possesses *sole* responsibility for supervising and evaluating all certified and noncertified personnel—those cited above. And while changes to school evaluations herein suggested will improve the quality of teacher evaluation processes, this improvement will not occur unless changes to the structuring of the position of principal are concurrently made.

As was described earlier, there is a relatively standard pathway by which one becomes a school principal. Teachers, having taught a prescribed number of years, earn master's degrees at the university level. Through meeting state-based certification requirements, they are then certified to become school principals. For principals wishing to rise higher in the education echelon, they attain degrees above the master's, typically PhD or EdD degrees.

And as common everywhere in today's public schools, one's advancement is largely enhanced by the number of university degrees obtained. Example: A teacher cannot become a *teacher of teachers*, a school principal, unless he/she checks off the box that states "master's degree." But as was described earlier, possession of a master's degree does not assure that the person in possession of such degree is an excellent teacher.

What is necessary in order for the paradigms presented here to be effective is *well-qualified* people in charge of, but not unilaterally performing, every one of the processes associated with teacher evaluations. And these people need to be dedicated to the purpose of performing just this *single* job, not so many other purely *administrative* school functions. In keeping with this format, there needs to be established the position of "principal" *exclusively* for the purpose of instructional leadership/teacher evaluation, to be a *distinct* entity in the school's leadership structure.

The currently constituted head of the school, the "principal," is replaced by a "chief executive officer," now the *head* of the school. Below this CEO will be a number of "principals." One of these will be charged exclusively with the role of instructional improvement/teacher evaluation. Other "principals" will attend other responsibilities, but not the responsibility of instructional supervision/teacher evaluation. Each other principal will be responsible for other aspects of school leadership, and all will report to the head of the school, the school's CEO.

The central reason for the creation of a unique "principal," one to serve *only* in the area of instructional supervision/teacher evaluation, is that this area is in need of far more attention than is available via current school organizational structures. As the number-one issue of importance, instructional supervision should receive the number-one priority attention it merits, via a position specifically and singularly dedicated to this function.

It should be noted that the precise *manner* of structural arrangement for the newly organized positions and function herein suggested may be different than stated. But the elevation of the instructional supervision/teacher evaluation function must be of paramount importance in any reorganization, whatever the other structural rearrangements might be. This "principal" position must be the first to be instituted in any administrative reorganization effort.

How the remaining functions are allocated and defined can be subject to more discussion, more than is necessary here. Here, the purpose is the elimination of the fraud of teacher evaluation, along with the ineptitude, conformity, and obfuscation that attends it in its current state of practice in the public schools. Raising the status of teacher evaluation through the suggestions outlined will go a long way toward achieving this end.

THE *QUINTESSENCE*:
MISSING IN ACTION IN THE PUBLIC SCHOOLS

Over fifty years ago, in October of 1966, a television show debuted that would become a classic, for young and old alike. *It's the Great Pumpkin, Charlie Brown* was a cartoon show featuring a group of child characters looking forward to Halloween.[36] One of these, Linus, ardently believed that on that night, the Great Pumpkin would rise out of the pumpkin patch and bring toys and goodies to all the children.

While his friends didn't believe him, Linus remained steadfast. He believed that sitting in the pumpkin patch on Halloween night, the most sincere one he was able to find in his neighborhood, he would see the Great Pumpkin rise up before him. And he understood why his friends did not believe. In a scene in the show, Linus mused that the reason his friends didn't believe in the Great Pumpkin was because it was, in today's language, politically incorrect to do so. He said, "There are three things I've learned never to discuss with people: religion, politics, and the Great Pumpkin."[37] And he was right!

Heeding the counsel of Linus, the Great Pumpkin will not enter into the discussion of teacher evaluation. And while some politically correct aspects of teacher evaluation have been explored, the topic of *religion* has remained untouched. Now it's time for religion, a "third-rail" topic, to be addressed. Taken directly from the New Testament of the Holy Bible, a statement written by the Apostle Paul has *substantial* importance in the matter of teacher evaluation:

And not only this, but we also exult in our tribulations, knowing that tribulation brings about perseverance . . . and perseverance, proven character; and proven character, hope. [38]

Very much in accord with what the ancient Greeks referred to as a *quintessence*, Paul's words are central to learning, teaching, and teacher evaluation today.

The ancient Greeks considered the world to be made up of earth, water, air, and fire—the "four essences." [39] A fifth essence, not found in the natural world, was labeled the "quintessence." This essence is defined as "the fifth and highest element in ancient and medieval philosophy that permeates all nature and is the substance composing the celestial bodies." [40] It is the essence of all four essences combined . . . but more!

THE QUINTESSENCE IN PUBLIC EDUCATION: WHAT MAKES LEARNING HAPPEN!

While most would see *tribulations* in a negative light, the Apostle Paul described them in a positive one. As tribulations often resulted in people becoming hopeful, he believed that they were to be exalted—"celebrated" in today's vernacular. As these pushed people to persevere, and through their perseverance generate positive states of character, they were a good thing! And while "tribulations" may be an antiquated term, tribulations remain ever present in the lives of people, and most certainly in the lives of young people in the public schools today.

In today's public schools, the *quintessence* of learning is students' motivation, students *wanting* to learn. Students' motivation to learn, combined with their attitudes toward learning, are the two most important issues in the public schools today. As such, they should be the *most* important issue in teaching, and teacher evaluation as well. But they are not. While these should be considered the quintessence in public education, they are often not given any attention at all.

At any level of schooling, students encounter difficulties in learning what their teachers are teaching. They experience tribulations. Some may experience small ones, minor difficulties in grasping a concept, meaning, or some other aspect of subject matter. Others find that they don't even know where to begin! In short, every student confronts times in their schooling when they have difficulties learning what's being taught by their teachers—experiencing tribulations therein.

And as was mentioned earlier, today's teachers, especially at the secondary level, serve as *dispensers* of content information, their unique subject matter. They do not dedicate much, if any, time to instructing their students about *how to learn* what they are teaching. In most public schools today, many students struggle to achieve success in their schooling because they have just never *learned how to learn*. They are given all the subject matter, but they don't know what to do with it in order to learn it. In another context, this would be like giving an automobile worker the parts of an automobile, but not instructions how to put them together to make a car.

As everyone knows, experiencing difficulties absent a pathway out of them can result in frustration, anxiety, and sometimes even anger. Too many students in the public schools today, not having the tools they need to do the jobs they are expected to do follows this same pathway. And a result, many will develop bad attitudes toward their schooling, resulting in low levels of motivation to succeed in their schooling. In addition to becoming unable to learn, some will then engage in behaviors, both in and outside of classrooms, that make the learning process difficult for others.

As any good football coach knows, a positive attitude motivates excellent performance. A positive attitude predisposes athletes to want to learn the skills they need to perform. In athletics, a successful performance is about two things: (1) performance skills; those techniques and behaviors that must be known and (2) attitudes; those mindsets that are needed to motivate athletes to learn the skills and techniques. In short, winning is an attitude, as is defeat. And *good* attitude can be taught!

TEACHING THE "HOW" . . . ALONG WITH THE "WHAT": WHAT COACHES DO—WHAT TEACHERS SHOULD DO ALSO

Athletic coaches spend a great deal of time teaching their athletes specific skill sets, the highly coordinated moves their athletes need to be able to make in order to win on the field of competitive play. This is the *stuff* of coaching, but it's only part of the stuff. The other part has to do with the manner in which their athletes approach the stuff, the athletes' attitude and motivation to learn the stuff. Coaches know that the first part can be achieved only if the second part is in place.

In high-level athletics today, in Big Ten football for example, the skill sets athletes bring to their coaches' programs are *all* going to be at a high level. Most athletes gaining full-ride scholarships to play football at any Big Ten university come with skills that are, with some notable exceptions, largely equivalent to the others who come. They are all top-tier athletes! But talent alone is not what will make for standout athletes.

Coaches know that the attitudes and levels of motivation will trump skill level development nearly *every* time. This is why coaches, as their athletes' *teachers*, dedicate a great deal of time to helping their athletes develop and maintain strong attitudes and positive-motivated mindsets. The same paradigm applies to other teachers, those teaching academic subjects in public schools for example. But unlike coaching, where skill sets are taught alongside attitude and motivation, the public schools have yet to engage this approach. And students are the losers!

MIA IN PUBLIC EDUCATION:
THE *QUINTESSENTIAL* MISSING CLASS

The K-12 curriculum in all public schools across the country comprises extensive lists of course offerings, some required and others elective. In the elementary grades, subject instruction is a secondary focus. The main curricular focus is reading, writing, and the ability to perform basic mathematical functions. In the secondary schools, courses are divided into various departments: sciences, language arts, social studies, mathematics, etc. Here the focus is on content learning in specific subject areas. But as routinely as schools offer a plethora of course offerings, they do not offer any classes in *learning how to learn*, as either required or elective.

Educators have known for a very long time that *attitude* and *motivation*, both in the category of "social and emotional" skills, are critical to learning. But few have taken the steps necessary to assure that these are taught to the students. These aspects of high-level student achievement, the quintessential elements of learning, are missing! These two student-engagement skills are not taught in the public schools, nor are they a significant part of principals' evaluations of their teachers. But why?

Teachers in public schools know some of their students will learn better than others, oftentimes because some come to school better equipped with the social and emotional skills needed for learning. And most teachers also know that their students' successes in school go well beyond that part of the curriculum they teach. Dr. Tara Laughlin, a contributor for the Academy for Social-Emotional Learning in Schools, suggests that what she terms "essential skills" are being left out of teaching:

> Academic knowledge is so last century. It is widely recognized that students need more than this to be successful later in life, especially in our diverse, ever-changing global landscape. Many additional skills are necessary to build well-rounded individuals prepared for college and careers. Social and emotional skills make up one category of these essential skills, including attributes such as *resiliency*, *stress management*, empathy, social awareness, and *self-confidence*. A systematic change in educational priorities is needed—one which affirms the reality that the world is different; one that grants social and emotional skills equal importance to traditional academic content; in other words, one which gives all students a real shot at success.[41] (emphasis mine)

These social and emotional skills, particularly those of *resiliency*, *stress management*, and *self-confidence*, are those that athletic coaches coach. These skills should be taught by classroom teachers as well! All having to do with engagement, they influence the degree to which focused and concentrated effort is brought to bear in learning. As *drivers* of the attitudes and degrees of motivation students generate, they are highly associated with students' success in school.

And while some might surmise that these skills should be emphasized mainly in the elementary grades, the study data provide information contradicting this view. Writing for the National Association of Independent Schools, Jonathan Martin and Amanda Torres point out that engagement training is *most* needed at the secondary levels of schooling:

Research indicates that student engagement declines as students progress from upper elementary grades to middle school, reaching its lowest levels in high school. Some studies estimate that, by high school, 40 to 60 percent of youth are disengaged. Given the serious consequences of disengagement, more and more educators and school administrators are interested in obtaining data on student engagement and disengagement for needs assessment, diagnosis, and preventative measures.[42]

While these data may seem surprising, they shouldn't be. As children grow and mature, their interests change dramatically. For years, psychologists have known that very young children are uniformly 100 percent *self*-absorbed. They see *themselves* as the center of the universe, and the universe is all about them! But as children age, their awareness shifts. Having transitioned into puberty, now to experience myriad socioemotional, hormonal-sexual, and body-image changes, they now experience the world around them as much more complicated.

Unlike when their focus of attention was almost uniformly self-centered, they now become increasingly influenced by what lies outside of who *they* are. Interests in a vast array of other things, things such as the opposite sex, now serve to distract their attention. And as these distractions grow in number and importance, they begin to replace the self-centered focus that engaged them in their childhood years. Almost overnight, Charlie has become more interested in *pitching* the girl sitting next to him in geometry class—more than the geometry *pitched* by his teacher. He has terrific engagement . . . it's just not in geometry!

While it should come as no surprise that Charlie is now less engaged in his schoolwork that he was in third grade, what is surprising is that school people are just now beginning to be interested in the change in Charlie! While educators seem predisposed with endless exercises in *data gathering*, athletic coaches have been incorporating this issue into their coaching strategies for a very long time. This information has been known for a long time, and they've been using it to the advantage of their players for a long time. But unlike coaches, teachers don't seem to have caught on to this powerful adjunct to learning.

For years, coaches have incorporated the seven ideal performance state (IPS) engagement principles of Dr. James Loehr: challenged, relaxed and calm, focused, excited with positive emotion, ready for fun and enjoyment, confident, automatic, and instinctive.[43] These *learned* principals, *taught* to athletes by their coaches, are what enable a football quarterback to calmly call the next play in front of thousands of screaming fans. What most football fans don't know is that this player doesn't even hear the crowd noise! Having learned to tune out this distraction, he is able to perform absent the damage it could cause him in playing *his* game. And just as a football player must have complete control over his game on a football field, a student must have complete control over his or her game in a classroom.

These same IPS strategies, those allowing a football player to tune out fan noise in a stadium, can also be used by students to tune out distractions in a classroom. But, as is true in coaching, the skill sets to accomplish this ability must be *taught*! Coaches coach them, and teachers should teach them! With all that is known about psychology, it is remarkable that educators do not routinely teach their students the skill sets needed to improve their performances in school, those that coaches teach their athletes to improve their performances in sports.

Success on the football field can translate to success in the classroom. Students need to receive the same kind of training that football players do. They should be receiving this in a class, or classes, offered by their schools. Classes wherein teachers teach these skills need to be incorporated into schools' curricula, as *required* subjects for *all* students. Accordingly, principals should be evaluating their teachers in these classes, just as they do in other classes taught in the schools. Teachers should be evaluated with regard to how effectively they incorporate these engagement strategies in their teaching. These strategies need to be reinforced continuously by teachers for their students, just as they are reinforced continuously by coaches for their players.

THEY WON'T *BUY* IT UNLESS YOU *SELL* IT!
THE TEACHER AS "SALESPERSON"

Too many teachers assume that students enter their classrooms because they want to learn what they have to teach. They are oftentimes wrong! Perhaps the insight that makes some teachers more effective than others is that unsuccessful teachers do not see themselves as *salespeople*. But teaching *is* about selling! It's about having a product that must be sold and finding a way that *makes* the consumer want to buy it. Teaching is about salesmanship!

In his paper, "On the Similarities between Teaching and Selling," Charles Wallfisch says it well: "Educators can learn more about the fundamentals of their work from business, with selling-buying and teaching-learning posited as equivalent transactions."[44]

In her paper "Teaching is Selling," lizTheDeveloper says:

> Most teachers are only able to get their students to retain 40% of the information they present, but I think this is due to the pitch. If people don't understand in context as to why it is important, their brains will neatly file it away under "not important," because that's what our brains are trained to do. However, if you *sell* the new information like it's a solution to a problem, our brains keep it top-of-mind for whatever that type of problem presents itself. It also lends itself to novel use better, because our brains try to pattern-match on problems, and whatever you're presenting is the solution for one problem, it might work for similar problems.[45]

What lizTheDeveloper presents as a *sales* device is nearly identical to what Dr. Robert Marzano presents as a *teaching* device called "pattern recognition."[46] Being nearly identical, these show how closely related the acts of teaching and selling really are.

Another who sees the interconnectivity between teaching and selling is Jack Malcolm, the president of Falcon Performance Group. A sales training organization, his organization is dedicated to improving the professionalism, preparation, and productivity of people in sales. He singles out the role that *persuasion* plays in both: "Persuasion often requires teaching, and teaching often requires persuasion. If you teach, think about doing a little more selling; if you sell, think about doing a little more teaching."[47]

The transfer of sales strategies to teaching heuristics in the public schools has been left out of teacher-training programs. Principals are also unschooled in these. As a result, they do not look for them as evidence of good teaching in their evaluations of their teachers. The skill sets that salespeople employ in their selling need to be incorporated into what teachers employ in their teaching. Similarly, principals need to be instructed in these so that they are properly equipped to evaluate their teachers' usage of them.

The application of sales techniques and the communication skills that inform them are two essential elements for teaching. But they have been overlooked in public education for decades. Experts in selling, those to be found in the business community, have not seen their expertise in selling incorporated into teacher- and principal-training programs at the universities. As a result, the expertise they have to offer has remained untapped by educators.

As a result, both teachers and principals are less adept in their respective fields—teachers teaching and principals evaluating their teaching. This needs to change! It's time that educators reached outside their relatively narrow fields of pedagogy to access what other workplace venues have to offer them. *Degree attainment*, that being substantially responsible for rising in the ranks in public education, is too often viewed by those in education to be the end-all and be-all in their profession. But the business of selling is a profession as well!

Many in education view "selling" as an inferiorly ranked activity as compared to their more lofty academic pursuits. This myopic, academically ethnocentric view of education needs to change! Some of the very best salespeople possess no degrees at all, but they know how to connect with people to make a sale! It is their ability to read people, knowing what will motivate a prospective buyer to want to buy a product, the one the salesperson wants to sell. It's very much akin to what a teacher must do to motivate a student to want to learn what the teacher is teaching. *The right stuff* comes in many forms!

THE RIGHT STUFF:
WHAT TEACHERS SHOULD BE TEACHING . . . AND
PRINCIPALS EVALUATING

The 1983 motion picture *The Right Stuff* dramatized the story of Tom Wolfe's best-selling book by the same name.[48] As in the book, the movie tells the story of the Navy, Marine, and Air Force test pilots involved in research for what would become America's first flight into space. Also told are the stories of the seven military pilots, those selected for Project Mercury, to be trained as pilots for this venture. These men were selected because their peers believed them to possess *the right stuff*, the unique characteristics that made them ideal for the challenges the mission would present.

In the public schools today, many students do not have *the right stuff*. And because they don't have it, the dropout rates in the public schools remain problematically high. While high school dropout rates have declined, they still remain high. A 2015 Child Trends report points to some of the reasons:

> A range of factors have been shown to increase a student's risk of dropping out, including high rates of absenteeism, *low levels of school engagement*, low parental education, work or family responsibilities, problematic or deviant behavior, moving to a new school in the ninth grade, and attending a school with lower achievement scores.[49] (emphasis mine)

While there are seven reasons that cause students to drop out, one has a substantial influence on the other six. Low levels of student engagement influence *all* the others! In other words, if a student could change his/her level of engagement from low to high, the other reasons for dropping out would diminish substantially. The effect would be that a heightened level of student engagement would provide the student a defense mechanism against the effects of the other six negative factors.

Due to these seven detractors, students have no *hope* for success. They will likely not *persevere* in their studies. As a result, they will not develop the *character* necessary to see them through the life challenges they have yet to face. As stated earlier, the Apostle Paul was right! Detractors, also known by the Apostle Paul as "tribulations," can be a positive energizer for engaging a student's performance. By failing to understand the prescience of Paul's words educators fail to provide their students *the right stuff*, those skill sets that coaches coach and teachers should be teaching.

The *hope* that Paul referenced was not born out of easy times, but out of tribulations. These same tribulations, those detailed in the Child Trends report, can be defeated when students are *taught* how to improve their engagement mechanisms for their schooling—when they come face-to-face with their own tribulations! It's well past time that teachers teach these skills and principals evaluate them. And while some might think this is a *new* field of work, first to require study and more research, they are wrong. The time is now! The tools have been around for a long time, and it's well past time that they be used in public school classrooms.

THE RIGHT CLASS FOR THE RIGHT STUFF: AN IPS (IDEAL PERFORMANCE STATE) CURRICULUM

As cited earlier, Drs. Robert Marzano and Daisy Arredondo developed a set of strategies for improving student learning.[50] Debuting in 1986 (over 30 years ago!), *Tactics for Thinking* largely remains gathering dust on educators' bookshelves. Their uniquely powerful program showed teachers how to teach their students *twenty-two* strategies (tactics) and how to use them to improve their thinking and learning abilities. While there are other approaches to get at these issues, the *Tactics* approach is one example of teaching students *the right stuff*!

But today, as teachers and their principals are wont to do, *Tactics for Thinking* has found no place in their school's curriculum. They just keep doing what they have always done, while simultaneously expecting a different result. It is not likely that teachers and their principals are displaying the signs of clinical insanity, as a now-famous quotation suggests: "The definition of insanity is doing the same thing over and over again and expecting different results."[51] But continuing to do what they've always done remains a fool's errand, especially when research continues to show the connection of engagement to learning.

But as was detailed earlier, teachers and their principals remain ensconced in a pervasive wave of teacher evaluation *rubrics* and checklists, largely generated by state-level department of education bureaucrats. In their quest to quantify what is most likely not quantifiable, via the checklist-laden rubrics, they generate reams of what constitutes little more than an agglomeration of *education-speak* compost—material thrown together that results in a decaying process of teacher evaluation.

And the proof, as it is said, is in the pudding! When asked, most teachers and their principals report that they give little attention to the checklists. They know that the checklists are wordy compositions of "educababble"! (No, it's not a *real* word, but an appropriately descriptive one nonetheless.) Because state departments of education mandate these data be submitted each year, teachers and principals dutifully comply.

In near lockstep conformity, teachers and principals squander time and energy, both of which should be brought to bear on a better system of teacher evaluation. Barring change, such as that which has been advocated herein, both will continue to miss what is perhaps the most apt measure of students' likelihood for success: the degree to which students are eager to engage in their schooling. This *quintessence* needs to be reintroduced to students, both via classes dedicated to teaching engagement strategies and the ongoing inculcation of these in their academic classes. And principals need to be in the forefront, seeing to it that this quintessential aspect of teaching performance becomes a part of their teacher evaluation process.

It should be noted that the changes to teacher evaluation processes herein suggested are not proposed as the *only* avenues to bring about positive change. There are likely other routes to change that can be explored. But change *is* needed, *substantial* change, if teaching performance in the public schools is to be assessed with accuracy and effectiveness.

What has been presented here is intended to make two points: (1) As currently constituted and carried out, teacher evaluation processes are both inaccurate and ineffective and (2) The central issues, the deficiencies cited herein, are resolvable, if those involved *choose* to change what needs to be changed. Thus far, aside from yearly cosmetic adjustments to teacher evaluation practices, the work of making the *meaningful* changes needed has yet to be engaged.

5

LEADERSHIP IN PUBLIC EDUCATION

The Missing Commodity

Instructional leadership in the public schools, centering on the building principal, has been the focus of discussion thus far. While commonly acknowledged as school leaders, do principals actually *lead*? Shown in the previous pages to be incapable of providing leadership in the area of instruction with teacher evaluation as the focus, there remain many other aspects of school operations wherein the principal's leadership is needed. But do they provide it? More succinctly, given the environments within which they work, *can* they provide it?

Are school principals truly the educational leaders in their buildings, those in charge of and seeing to the ongoing quality of all educational activities in their schools? Those in the education coterie have advanced this proposition for decades—but is it true? And if they are not, what do they do all day? Might they mostly occupy themselves with *administrative* tasks, those not directly associated with the nuts and bolts of teaching and learning? That's what the role of the building principal was when first introduced, so is it the same today?

As was said earlier, school principals are not under attack here. As is true for any grouping of people, most are wonderfully kind and responsible people, wanting only to do a good job in what they are assigned. What is in question here is neither their integrity nor their desire to do a good job. What is in question is whether or not they *can* do their jobs, the *leadership* roles they are assigned, given the way their jobs are currently constituted. In order to address this issue, the paradigm of analogy will provide a means of delving into the issues that impact the jobs school principals are asked to do—jobs that are almost *undoable* as they are currently constituted.

The leadership role played by Mayor Rudy Giuliani, acting in the aftermath of the attack on the World Trade Center on September 11, 2001, is here compared with the role of the school principal, acting in the conduct of daily school activities. As is true of all analogies, this one is not a one-to-one (apples-to-apples) paradigm. But the *roles* of leadership lend themselves to an accurate and fair comparative assessment, one sufficient to make the point intended.

Some will think that this comparison is not apropos, but it is. Mayor Rudy Giuliani intervened to save people's lives, many of which would have been lost in the absence of his intervening leadership. Principals act on saving their students' lives, but not their *physical* lives. Principals intervene to save the lives of their students, those that will become lost absent a principal's intervening leadership. Students failing to gain the enrichment of a quality education will experience their lives being "lost" due to ignorance. Those lives will be lost in that they will be *acted on* by life's circumstances, rather than being lives that are capable of *acting on* life's circumstances. The difference is about living purposeful lives, not reactive lives.

While the analogy isn't perfect, it's close enough so that some valid points of comparison can be made. Being made, they will show why principals' leadership roles are both grossly exaggerated and inaccurate with regard to what the education coterie would have citizens *believe*. Unfortunately, as is stated in the epilogue, some people would much rather *believe* than *know*! Through positing this comparison, perhaps some may become better able to *know*.

LEADERSHIP IN PUBLIC EDUCATION: NO LEADERS NEED APPLY!

On September 11, 2001, Mayor Rudy Giuliani and his staff were faced with the task of addressing an attack on New York City that was, in terms of American deaths, worse than that of Pearl Harbor on December 7, 1941. How he and his staff managed the issues presented on that day is detailed in the first chapter of his book *Leadership*. How they performed on that day and on those that followed can be described as nothing short of selfless and heroic.

With countless hours addressing ever-evolving situations, it became apparent to his staff, those people that Giuliani brought on board early in his term as mayor, that his unique leadership style would pay huge dividends. For a moment, consider the result of a similar effort under similar circumstances, but this time managed and conducted by employees (teachers and principals) of the public schools. It would have looked quite different!

Rescue and recovery efforts were severely impaired due to constraints imposed on the work effort:

1. All rescue and recovery work was confined to the previously agreed-upon workday time frame.
2. A guaranteed daily period of time for making plans (a planning period), within the regular workday, was required; no other activity could infringe upon this time period.
3. The number of daily work tasks assigned to each worker was limited via a previously agreed-upon quantity.
4. After-hours work would not be expected nor demanded from any worker engaged in the rescue-recovery effort. If such should become inevitable, compensation time would be granted at a later date.
5. Task accomplishment was slow and often lacking due to leadership's failure to direct operations at the site. Three deficiencies were noted: First, supervisors did not appear to know what to do. Seeking guidance from committees of their peers slowed operations. Second, supervisors were noticeably reticent to issue directives. Third, the workforce maintained a highly cohesive opposition to being directed; it slowed operations by insisting that directives be negotiated.

This is a harsh assessment perhaps, but likely an accurate one nonetheless. Were the staffers of Mayor Giuliani performing to the standards of teachers in today's public schools, this would have been the likely result. The reason for this is that an organization that controls the behaviors of the workforce would not have allowed that force (teachers and administrators in this make-believe scenario) the free hand to do what needed to be done. The name of that organization? The National Education Association.

The NEA, its state affiliates, and their local adjuncts conspire to set, with exceedingly fine precision, the working conditions, workday time frames, benefits, etc., for teachers in the public schools. In this contrived storyline, a made-up tale of teachers staffing a 9/11 rescue and recovery operation, the NEA would have proven to be a constraint sufficient to hamper a successful effort. The "master agreement" would not have allowed for what was needed. But even more important in closing the circuit of failure in this circumstance would have been the resistance, even the refusal, of leadership to perform its main function: that of *leading*.

This is *not* to say that the public school teachers would not have had the intrinsic courage, conviction, or desire to perform admirably, as did those under the leadership of Rudy Giuliani. That would be a false assumption. However, it *is* to say that the teachers' "negotiated contract" would have precluded such a performance. Nor does this story suggest that the leadership was without the prerequisite *desire* to respond either. While *wanting* to lead, principals would also know that their abilities were not up to what was required. They would know, as they suspected their teachers would, that their ineptitude rendered them unable to perform their leadership functions.

In *Leadership*, Rudy Giuliani details several leadership rules that are not applicable in the public schools. Excellent rules as they are, they cannot be applied in the public schools because of the lemming-like compliance of the workforce, teachers and administrators, with NEA-negotiated work regulations. School superintendents and school principals, ostensibly those in positions of leadership, cannot and do not lead because the public school environment does not support leadership—at least not of a kind that Mayor Giuliani employed on September 11.

In addition to the National Education Association, there exist many others who exert their influence upon both teachers and administrators, those being the members of the education coterie previously discussed. Activist groups, professional organizations representing administrators, exert a new force in public education, the force of political correctness, in both thought and behavior. And all these influencing entities have learned how the game is played, how to retain their respective positions of influence in the public schools. Even textbook companies have figured out the rules!

Once every year the NEA Representative Assembly meets in convention, but there is in attendance a paucity of textbook publishers. The reason: "Publishers have apparently learned from experience that— apart from ensuring that textbooks take the politically correct line on racism, homophobia, etc., etc.—no one at the Representative Assembly is actually interested in education."[1]

In this made-up circumstance wherein public school staffers would be called upon to perform rescue and recovery after 9/11, they could not perform because they were not *allowed* to perform. The organization largely responsible for defining their workday activities, the NEA, ignored the reality of the tasks to be accomplished in deference to their controlling interests in the workforce. Similarly, public school employees, both teachers and administrators, cannot accomplish the work of educating young people, and for the same reason.

The NEA ignores the task of educating children in deference to its control of the workforce charged with this responsibility, with the willing complicity of that workforce. And principals and superintendents, the supposed agents of leadership, remain passively, conformingly compliant. Some examples playing out within the public school venue, contrasted with Mayor Giuliani's approach, will reveal how this comes about.

CHAPTER 5, *LEADERSHIP*:
"SURROUND YOURSELF WITH GREAT PEOPLE"

When Rudy Giuliani took office on the January 1, 1994, his first task was to install a staff of *his* choosing to conduct business. His process was not complicated. "I tried to visualize who would be at my meetings, to picture who I would like to have around me and how those people would interact with one another. I wanted amiable team builders and ornery contrarians. Above all, I sought to match the best person available to the job best suited for that person."[2]

Contrast this with the circumstance in any public school district at any level of leadership, in this case the school principal. The new principal arrives at his/her new assignment, finding that nearly *all* the staff is already in place. Many of these people will likely have been in their positions for years, having their *own* ways of doing things. Some will be openly opposed to accommodating any changes. Others will contest change in a more covert manner, by conspiring with a group of colleagues all well known to them, but unknown by the new principal.

Even the closest of staff members, the principal's secretarial and administrative assistants, are in place and have their own agendas. Perhaps the assistant principal, supposed to be the principal's closest ally, was among those who applied, and was rejected, for the position the new principal now occupies. Given these circumstances, why would a new principal make the assumption that these people stand at the ready to implement a new leadership plan . . . that of a new person, and outsider to all?

In *Winning the Future*, Newt Gingrich makes an assessment that is directly applicable to public school education: "There should be a lot more thought given to changing personnel laws so leaders can arrive in a new assignment with a core team of people they are used to working with."[3] Does this occur anywhere in public education, and would anyone wish to give odds that the NEA would support this?

While principals face this situation in every K-12 public school building in every school district, consider the even greater impact for the very top leader in public school districts, the superintendent of schools. For this person, the pervasiveness of this situation is district-wide! This leader also has no option to select those with whom he/she will seek to govern. *All* downline leaders and their staffs, the district's principals and teachers, are past players with their own agendas, not necessarily congruent with the new leader's visions for the district.

And while forthright opposition might not be the strategy chosen by most, a more subtle passive aggressiveness by some might suffice to derail any substantive success to be achieved by the new superintendent. For parents, boards of education, and educators to maintain that *real* leadership can be exercised under these conditions is tantamount to what William Bennett references as "normalized falsification."[4] The outcome is that people may not really *believe* that leadership is happening, but they behave as though they do while ignoring the evidence that it is not.

CHAPTER 9, *LEADERSHIP:* "BE YOUR OWN MAN"

Mr. Giuliani says, "if you're doing your job and putting your motives and conscience through their paces, accept that maybe you do really know better and can see a little further down the road than others."[5] And if one is to lead, or "show the way,"[6] one must be reasonably sure that one *knows* the way. *Knowing* is the bedrock of a person being his or her own person. Absent this, a leader is virtually held hostage by the thoughts and whims of present company. Knowing is the critical prerequisite for the exercise of leadership. As Dr. McFarland says, "There's no substitute for knowing."[7]

One might reasonably expect then that a board of education would place a high premium on hiring a superintendent who has strong content knowledge (knowing) about teaching children. This board would also expect that their superintendent would lead through the application of this knowing to conditions resident in the school district, resulting in improvement in the teaching/learning process therein. While this is an excellent leadership format for the public schools, there is a problem with that "knowing" part. It's absent!

Knowing is absent because teacher-training institutions turn out ill-prepared products (teachers), those who do not possess adequate content knowledge within the areas of their subject expertise. Virtually *all* leaders in the public schools, department heads, principals, begin their careers in public education as teachers. Thus, the perpetuation of this knowledge deficit rises inexorably upward as these people move upward through the leadership ranks, ultimately to the position of superintendent of schools.

Notwithstanding the acquisition of a variety of additional education degrees awarded by the same teacher-training institutions, and with the recognition that some exceptions exist, content-deficient leaders (principals and superintendents) are more likely the rule than the exception. In his "Bill of Indictment" of public education, Martin Gross tells why this is the case:

1. The licensing of teachers, what is known as certification, is a ritual without substance, requiring knowledge at the lowest possible level.

2. Teacher training is lax. The undergraduate degree of most teachers, usually a bachelor of education, is less substantial than any
ordinary liberal arts degree. The same hollowness is true of the
master's degree obtained by teachers.
3. The doctor of education degree, the Ed.D., held by most school
superintendents and administrators, is inferior to the traditional
Ph.D. degree and requires little academic knowledge.[8]

Superintendents, occupying the highest positions of leadership in
public schools, may represent the best caricature of the Peter Principle.[9] According to this paradigm, a person rises up through any hierarchical organization until reaching his/or her level of incompetence. As
examples of this principle, superintendents largely perform management functions, those disguised as *educational leadership*, whether or
not they acknowledge that their ineptitude moves them to do so. And
while true *leadership* is markedly absent in the conduct of this management function, tolerance is its hallmark!

With management, not leadership, as the focus, it is no surprise that
today's public school leaders have difficulty defining any action or belief
system as "right" or "wrong." The politically correct "thinking" overlay
that *all* ideas must be perceived as equal, be they erudite or nonsensical, is the accepted philosophy in the public schools today. As Dennis
McCallum, the author of *The Death of Truth*, states, "The extreme
reluctance of postmodern educators to judge, test, and evaluate seems
destined to produce occupationally inept people who can't handle being
told they are wrong."[10]

As another example of this atmosphere of permissiveness, teachers
are taught to avoid damaging students' self-esteem by labeling their
responses "incorrect." Instead of simply stating that a student has given
an incorrect answer, teacher-training institutions now teach teachers to
offer *kinder* options: "Um-hmmm," "That's a thought," "That's one possibility," "That's one idea," "That's another way of looking at it," "I hear
you,"[11] and other non sequiturs employed to obscure the fact that a
wrong answer was given.

Not only do teachers placate students via this kinder-gentler approach, administrators deal with their staffs in this same manner, not
wanting to run the risk of being viewed as judgmental, or worse yet,
authoritarian! After all, at least for building principals, teachers will

typically evaluate their principals in writing, usually anonymously. And these evaluations will likely be reviewed by their principal's boss, the superintendent of schools.

Being one's own man, or one's own woman, is not a salable trait in public education for public school principals. Teachers are not comfortable with strident leadership exhibited by principals. And principals have come to know that *getting along* is a better way. Conforming to commonly accepted group-think is better for one's survival than is independent thinking. This is well illustrated by Professor Todd Whitaker. Professor Whitaker is an ASCD (Association for Supervision and Curriculum Development) author. Bearing in mind that this organization is a part of the *education coterie*, it should come as no surprise that Dr. Whitaker advocates *getting along* as a leadership paradigm to be adopted by those he teaches in his university classes and seminars.

In referencing school principals and their decision-making functions, Dr. Whitaker says, "Base *every* decision you make on your best teachers. If my best teachers don't think that something is a good idea, what are the chances that it is a good idea?"[12] (emphasis mine). Dr. Whitaker represents the currently in-vogue belief of many teacher-training institutions that consensus is *always* preferable to independent decision-making. As a result of the mindset promoted by Dr. Whitaker and many others, principals are schooled into believing that their proper role is choreography, not leadership.

And while Dr. Whitaker advocates for his "the more heads the better" approach to leadership, he avers from mentioning the most important matter for many school principals who adopt this approach: the CYA factor! A *Time* magazine cover story of several years ago cautioned readers to "Be Worried, Be Very Worried."[13] While this story was referencing the topic of "global warming," it might just as easily have been referencing school principals, those concerned that their decision-making might lead to their seeking new employment opportunities. For these, the wide dispersal of decision-making that Dr. Whitaker promotes is tailor-made for their job security interests. Should things go awry, spreading decision-making responsibility is well adapted to spreading blame as well.

However, it would be grossly unfair to portray school principals as inordinately fearful without showing simultaneously that they are largely justified in their trepidations. In fact, principals' anemic leadership, that which avoids taking positions unpopular with teachers (and students), can be viewed as justifiable given the conditions under which they work. Some of their workplace realities are as follows.

Unlike teachers, principals have no *tenure* in their positions. Principals are contracted on a year-to-year basis. As such, they have no certitude for employment beyond the year in which they are serving at any point in time. Superintendents achieve a measure of job security in that they are hired, typically, with multiyear contracts.

As previously mentioned, teachers, and sometimes students, play an important role in the *yearly* evaluation of the principal's performance. Most often, these evaluations are done anonymously. Principals are often under an obligation to provide the results of these evaluations with their bosses.

"School climate" has become a strong measuring stick by which a school's leadership functions are evaluated. A poor *climate* is often viewed by superintendents and boards of education as a sign of the principal's poor leadership skills.

A further word about "school climate" is in order, so as to portray just how powerful this issue has become in the lives of school principals. In the 1960s, Rensis Likert advanced his theory of *participatory management*.[14] In 1981, William Ouchi published his book *Theory Z: How American Management Can Meet the Japanese Challenge*.[15] The Association for Supervision and Curriculum Development, a member of the heretofore-referenced education coterie, trumpeted these new theories of management to educators across the country. "School climate" became the most talked-about subject in public education, rising in stature so as to impact the criteria by which principals across the country were evaluated.

Over time, the result of this veritable *school climate* stampede was that schools with happy teachers, not prone to complaint, lack of cooperation, or other such behaviors, were seen as those schools having highly effective principals. This paradigm has retained considerable staying power in public schools as well as colleges of education to this day. School principals are well aware that their schools, and their leadership status, are viewed through this narrow evaluation lens.

Given the strong staying power of the school climate movement in public education, it becomes most reasonable for principals to watch their *Ps and Qs* when dealing with their teachers. Avoidance of confrontation becomes a mode of behavior for school principals, and most would certainly not choose to act in accord with the words of James Bryant Conant. A master chemist who rose in academic ranks to become the president of Harvard University, he wrote, "Behold the turtle. He makes progress only when he sticks his neck out!"[16] When the quality of a school principal's performance is measured with a school climate yardstick, turtles become soup!

CHAPTER 4, *LEADERSHIP*:
"EVERYONE'S ACCOUNTABLE, ALL OF THE TIME"

In any so-called final analysis, the question of who gets the credit, or blame, for the public education circumstance is a legitimate one to ask: To what degree are the schools successful in educating young people and who is responsible? When he was mayor of New York City, a sign on Rudy Giuliani's desk read, "I'm Responsible!"[17] It would be unlikely that any school district employee, particularly in a leadership role, would be sporting such a sign on their desk. In today's public schools, teachers are not assessed via any real/concrete systems of *knowing*. Administrators (principals and superintendents) are assessed more on their political skills than their educational acumen. Parents have no part in an assessment of anything. With this kind of process in place, it is difficult to find *data-based* answers pertaining to the reasons why success or failure occurs, and particularly about who or what might be responsible.

As previously stated, the 1983 *A Nation At Risk* study provided several substantive recommendations to correct the deficits it identified.[18] However, rather than apply those soundly arrived-at recommendations, the public education establishment (to include all of its *education coterie* participants) continues to persevere with studies and committees formed for the purpose of developing new truths, examples of which are legion: whole language instruction, the new mathematics, students' portfolio compilations, values clarification exercises, and multicultural education-based strategies are but a few of these. In following the newest fads and/or trends, those that comport well with contemporary political correct ideologies, solid *knowledge-based* content and pedagogical skills are left wanting.

While educators, many of whom inhabit university colleges of education, succeed in reinventing the wheel, they ultimately find that "round" still works best! In his writings about education in his native England in 1910, G. K. Chesterton was prescient in describing what public education in 21st-century America has become: "The trouble in too many of our modern schools is that the State, being controlled so specially by the few, allows cranks and experiments to go straight to the schoolroom when they have never passed through the Parliament, the public house, the church, or the marketplace."[19]

The aversion of public school educators to take responsibility akin to the sign on Mayor Giuliani's desk is reinforced by the education coterie, what American historian Arthur Bestor defined as the "interlocking public school directorate."[20] A bureaucracy of bureaucracies, Bestor references the static nature of this group: "One of the most shocking facts about the field of education is the almost complete absence of rigorous criticism from within."[21] There is little doubt that a palpable disquiet exists between teachers and administrators in the normal run of any school day. But they close ranks quickly when their common ground is called into question by outsiders, those non-coterie members—parents in particular, those who might question their policies or actions.

In such a circumstance, principals and teachers *circle the wagons* in their common defense of whatever is happening in the school, even when inappropriate behaviors come to light. Recall the "white privilege test" given to students by Wisconsin middle school teachers. While their behavior was inappropriate and in violation of district policy, their principal indicated that he would not take any action against them.[22] This incident serves to portray well the lack of rigorous criticism from within referenced by Mr. Bestor.[23] And as the Wisconsin scenario displays, parental complaints can get the attention of school leaders, but little results when leaders refuse to lead.

CHAPTER 13, *LEADERSHIP*: "STUDY, READ, LEARN INDEPENDENTLY"

"Any good leader must develop a substantive base. No matter how talented your advisors and deputies, you have to attack challenges with as much of your own knowledge as possible."[24] The ability, desire, and purposefulness of those educators who follow this paradigm is what allows them to rise above the malaise of what is described herein, thus making substantial contributions in educating children. They make a difference primarily because they choose to go beyond their formal university preparation programs to find answers, contest nonsense, and lead from a substantive base of content knowledge and pedagogy. But in an ever-increasing climate of political correctness, that driven by those "progressives" striving to reduce educational vibrancy to their doctrinaire mindsets, their numbers are shrinking.

Those who exercise *real* leadership behavior, that not in keeping with the education coterie's orthodoxy, often draw fire from others, even their own colleagues. One such was a teacher in California, regarded by his colleagues as an interfering fanatic. He violated the rules of the contract. He reported teachers who were selling real estate in the teacher's lounge or calling in sick to extend their weekends. He was so hated by union officials that they circulated a celebratory note when he left the school district. "We got him out," it read. The teacher's name: Jaime Escalante—whose achievements in teaching calculus to inner-city Hispanic students led Hollywood to produce a film about him, *Stand and Deliver*.[25]

Escalante was aside and apart from those union/teacher colleagues, those who criticized him for his unorthodox behavior. His choice to read, study, and learn about his students, that which allowed him to teach them effectively, brought him into conflict with his colleagues and their coterie dogma. Notwithstanding his success with his students, the price for his behavior was a severe estrangement from his colleagues. Today, as was true in Escalante's time, substantive successes in teaching and learning are directly related to the degree to which educators cast off the group-think of the education coterie, the pervasive lingua franca of public education.

Of no small consequence for public education outcomes is the necessity that leaders reassert their roles of *leading*. Merely coordinating the activities of others, as was true of principals in the 1800s, does not serve the needs of 21st-century schooling. Such constitutes school administration, but not school leadership. While consensus-building, cooperative decision-making, collaboration, and other group dynamics should continue to play a role in a principal's leadership repertoire, *real* leaders assert their authority beyond the dictates of collectivist activities. An effective educational leader must fly in the face of coterie dogma, asserting that the public schools must be 100 percent *democratic* in their conduct of business.

The late Robert Bork stated this matter succinctly: "the spread and triumph of the democratic ideal leads, irrationally, to the belief that inequalities are unjust so that hierarchical institutions must be democratized."[26] School superintendents and principals, if they are to lead in a Giulianian sense, must reinsert themselves back into the educational process by directing the teaching workforce, not merely administering it.

This role was vacated decades ago. It will not be an easy task for principals and superintendents to reinstate themselves into their rightful roles, given the prevailing get-along milieu in schools today. As Robert Bork reminded, "The idea that democracy and equality are not suited to the virtues of all institutions is a hard sell today."[27] No doubt, in their clamor to achieve more and more power to influence (read: "lead") the public education process, teachers and their NEA consorts will ensure that principals and superintendents will, indeed, have a very *hard sell* in regaining the leadership responsibilities assigned them.

As Rudy Giuliani knows and has demonstrated, a leader can ill afford to disperse authority until it is so thinly constituted that it disappears loosely into the workforce ostensibly being led. This is a lesson that school leaders have seemingly failed to learn. The extent to which any will be successful in leading in the future will be related to how closely they follow the advice given by the late General Norman Schwarzkopf: "When placed in command, take charge."[28]

WILL/CAN LEADERS RESUME LEADING?
WHO *ARE* THE LEADERS?

At the outset, an analogy was drawn between the 9/11 attack on New York City and how the rescue operations would have gone if conducted by public school personnel. As has been shown, it would not have gone well—clearly not as well as the Giuliani-run operation. The performance difference in this example allows for the obvious differences in training for those performing the duties of rescue and recovery. It should go without saying that no one would expect teachers and school principals to be capable of doing what skilled rescue personnel could do.

The intent of the analogy is to show how public school employees, given the union-ethic organization and resident leadership deficits, would have/could have addressed the tasks. In short, as they are currently constituted, they would not have been able to cope with the disaster at hand. In concluding this made-up paradigm, how does the state of public schooling bear a resemblance to on-the-ground realities present on September 11, 2001? It is simply this: Through the assessment of its current performance as was provided in the preceding pages, it is likely that many people consider public education to be in a state of existential "disaster."

INSTRUCTIONAL LEADERSHIP: THE *WHAT* AND THE *HOW*

If public schools are to regain their primary role of providing the country an educated populace, the first order of business needs to be that teachers become better accomplished in two areas: They must be found to be teaching academically correct and proper material in their classrooms, and they must be found to be teaching it effectively—teaching it well.

In order to assure parents and others that these metrics are being accomplished, principals must become proficient, *far* more so than they currently are, in making these determinations. To do so, principals will need to adopt new *knowing-based* criteria for assessing teacher competencies, moving away from the currently employed *visual* processes—what good teaching *looks like.*

In an age wherein America is in a worldwide competition with other rapidly developing countries, one wherein it is currently not *winning*, American schools must be teaching their students not only *what* to know, but *how* to know it, and teach *both* better! The suggestions for beginning this process must be engaged sooner than later if America is to escape the current educational malaise in which it is currently mired.

If American public schooling is to remain the main avenue for educating *all of the children of all of the people*, such as was its first charter, it must change its management structure. School principals must engage new strategies, those that will enable them to perform the role of *instructional* leadership, the role they have tacitly come to accept but cannot accomplish. As has been suggested, they must go beyond their own limited knowledge bases, seeking that which they do *not* know from those who *do* know. To become effective school *leaders*, principals must do more than merely continue to rearrange the deck chairs on the sinking ship!

SOCIETAL/CULTURAL LEADERSHIP: THE *WHY*

Improving the teaching of solid content knowledge to students, and teaching it better, represents but one half of what will result from the resumption of reinvigorated leadership in the public schools. Students' understandings of content knowledge are of use only if these can be put to use in a *viable* culture. That culture must be underpinned with strong moral, ethical, and academically honest principles of behavior— a culture that promotes open and intellectually honest discussion of the issues confronting it. A culture that supports such is the second half of why a resumption of leadership is of such high importance in the public schools. Such a culture cannot be defined by, nor subject to the whims of, special-interest groups, many of which place their destructive interests above those of the larger culture.

These groups, many of whose aims are largely radically aberrant, must not be allowed to dominate the culture. Moreover, they cannot be given a free hand to dominate the culture's educational institutions, the public schools. The public schools serve as leveling agents, those that *maintain* the American culture in its most time-treasured institutions. The writers of the American Constitution instilled these into the American culture, and they are largely found in the Ten Commandments of the Christian Holy Bible.

Collectively, these ten *behavioral* precepts make the American culture what it is! They also continue to serve as the foundation for what the culture may become, determining its direction and even its future existence. But do they remain applicable in today's modern times? Or are these now things that might have applied when the country was founded, but are now outdated? And what about that *religious* part? Isn't that out of date today?

If one is 100 percent secularist, the Ten Commandments may seem to be inappropriate teachings for public schools, not at all what should be taught as culturally sustaining. But only *four* of these make any reference to God or any other entity that one might deem some form of deity.[29] In his book, *The Ten Commandments: Still the Best Moral Code*, Dennis Prager shows why the last six commandments, all what might be termed *religion-neutral*, remain excellent standards for behavior in the American culture.[30]

While precluding the negative acts of murder, adultery, theft, false testimony, and craving the possessions of others, the positive act of bestowing honor on parents completes these six cultural *rules of the road*. Whether attributed to the Mind of God or extraterrestrial alien carvings on ancient rocks, it matters not! As they have been for centuries, these six remain excellent rules to live by, both for individuals and societies! It's well past time that educators rediscover them and take steps to reincorporate them into classroom teaching activities in the public schools. There is no "separation of religion and state" involved!

In addition to leadership asserting itself into the arena of *what* is being taught, and *how* it is being taught, leadership must reassert itself into the teaching of these six precepts. As was previously asked, what value is there in *knowing* the right stuff if one doesn't *have* the right stuff, in order to *implement* the right stuff? To attain the complete *package*, three groupings of people will need to reclaim some very meaningful roles, ones that they have either forgotten or forsaken in the past. In so doing, a newly invigorated leadership by all three will be essential!

THE ESSENTIAL TRIUMVIRATE: THE *WAY*

The three groups, the *essential triumvirate* of people reengaging with the schools to achieve the *what, how,* and *why*, are these: school administrators, the colleges of education that train them, and the parents whom both purport to serve. Among these, parents are the *most* important! Absent *active* leadership emanating from parents, both from individual parents and collectives of parents, nothing of substance will change in the public schools!

If parents do not seize their responsibility for what is happening in their schools, they will remain little more than what they have become over the past several decades: passive recipients of whatever their schools choose to provide them. And their children will suffer the most meaningful losses. It all *must* begin with the parents, and some have already begun to see the light.

A POSITIVE OUTCOME FROM A TRAGIC EVENT: PARENTING OUTSIDE THE HOME

On February 14, 2018, a former student of Florida's Marjory Stoneman Douglas High School snuffed out the lives of fourteen students and three staff members during a shooting rampage. And while this tragic event was a result of a confluence of many failures in leadership, the failed leadership of the school district's leaders cannot, and should not, be underestimated. Those in charge, standing in loco parentis (in the place of parents), failed to lead in their *most* important role: assuring and protecting the safety of students!

Edmund Burke, an Irish statesman in the 1700s, is sometimes quoted when matters of leadership come into conversations. His leadership paradigm was simple: "The only thing necessary for the triumph of evil is for good men to do nothing."[31] While Burke referenced *men*, it's clear that his leadership paradigm applies to *women* as well. Two parents, one a woman, appear to have taken Burke's statement to heart. Both have chosen to step up to assert *their* leadership in the aftermath of tragedies that had impacts not only on their lives, but moreover on the lives of others in the community where they live.

> Two parents of students shot and killed at Marjory Stoneman High School in Parkland, Florida are running together for two seats on the Broward County School Board, Politico is reporting. Lori Alhadeff lost her 14-year-old daughter, Alyssa, in the mass shooting at the school. Ryan Petty's 14-year-old daughter, Alaina, died in the shooting. Seventeen people were murdered in the Feb. 14 shooting spree and another 17 were injured.

Both Alhadeff and Petty say they want to bring more security, accountability, and transparency to the school system, Politico noted.

"I don't want Alyssa's life to be in vain," Alhadeff told Politico. "I'm doing this because I don't want another parent to go through the pain and anguish that I have to go through every day."

"If I don't get in there and change it, it's unlikely to change," Petty said. "And we'll end up continuing the same approach that clearly failed at Marjory Stoneman Douglas."[32]

While Ryan Perry referenced "the same approach that failed at Marjory Stoneman Douglas,"[33] a *policy reason* that caused this tragic event, he was being unnecessarily kind. While it is true that the policies in place were insufficient in the protection they afforded children, it is *people* who formulated the policies who are responsible for their failure. Key people failed in their leadership roles to put in place the *right* policies.

Both the Florida school superintendent and the school principal are participant-members in what has been described as the *education coterie*, also defined as the *interlocking school directorate*. As the ostensible "leaders" in the school community, they failed to put in place policies that could have prevented the tragic events on February 14. But as has been shown to be the case in most of the coterie, they failed to lead effectively. As a result, two parents have come forward to take on a leadership role in the school district. And whether or not they will be able to effect meaningful change in their schools, their actions show how *very* important parents are in public education.

The message of this tragic event is hard to miss: The public schools are subject to the control and governance of the parents! And while these two parents have stepped forward in their attempt to bring *their* leadership to bear, far too many other parents, not having suffered such grievous losses, remain on the sidelines of their children's educations. They fail to play *any* role in the daily events taking place in their children's schools, those having the capacity to harm them both physically and academically.

While not being about every parent seeking a position on the local school board, every parent should make a point to be *actively involved* in what their school boards are doing— those things directly affecting their children's educations. With all the things taking place in the public schools recently, things that would have commonly been thought absurd in the past few years, it is not difficult to find examples wherein parents *should* become involved. And some situations are *so* far out of mainstream thinking that they are not even close calls!

Most parents, likely in extraordinarily high numbers, would not agree that their children, male and female, use the *same* bathrooms, or dress in the *same* locker rooms, or play on the *same* sports teams. However, they have been silent in making their wishes known to their school boards. Perhaps cowed by the radical activists who push these radical agendas, they have stayed in the shadows. Parents must change, if they want their schools to change.

First, parents must take an *active* role in seeing to it that those people elected to their school boards are those who represent *their* interests, not the interests of a small but loud-voiced minority. Once these board members are placed in office, parents must attend enough school board meetings to make sure that their wishes are carried out. "Enough school board meetings" means the number of meetings necessary to make sure that board members are performing their duties properly, in keeping with that which *parents* deem right and appropriate.

While some matters of public education are rightly within the province of the "professionals," the teachers, counselors, and school district administrators, far too many matters have been coopted by these three groups in recent years. Too many of these are in areas within which they have no business operating. Parents must remain vigilant in supervising the supervisors they elected, their board of education members, to be sure that their parenting roles are not usurped.

Casting aside the oftentimes unproductive PTA meetings, those that most parents do not attend, parents need to form *new* organizations. These organizations, one within every school, attend to matters that affect their children's educations. Each school also sends one of its members to serve on a district-wide organization. In these, parents need to *lead* in three venues: First, they must attend to the things that happen in their children's schools, those matters affecting their children on a day-to-day basis. Second, they must elect people to their school boards who represent *their* wishes. Third, they must make sure that they stay informed about what their elected representatives are doing, making sure that these are carrying out *their* wishes: those for which they were elected.

Parents must regain and reassert their leadership roles in their public schools, those roles that they have allowed their school officials to usurp. As was described in the historical perspective detailed in chapter 1, a system of checks and balances was the first format for public schooling in America. Schools and parents worked together, collaborating in their efforts for the education of the children. Neither school people nor parents thought it proper to take or override the role of the other, imposing its will against the wishes of the other. But that has changed in recent years as school people have increasingly substituted their beliefs and practices for those of the parents.

In this *new dynamic*, who is to ensure that the wishes of parents are heeded? What *leadership* is in place to see to it that this takes place? What about those school officials, the superintendents and principals?

SUPERINTENDENTS AND PRINCIPALS: DO EITHER LEAD?

As is true for almost every principal in the country, the positions they occupy are mostly about their performance of administrative matters, those set in place well before they assumed their jobs. While most people think the positions of their school principals and superintendents are "leadership" positions, they are not. While these positions may be structured to be such in a district's organizational chart, they are not such in how they are performed in the day-to-day operations of schools. Regarding school leadership, when it's all said and done, there's more said than done!

And while *school* people from all corners of the education coterie speak prolifically about principals being leaders of their schools, they are not speaking about a boots-on-the-ground reality. And while school superintendents are designated to be leaders at the *district* level, it is the school principals who are charged with leading their schools, thus carrying out the district's overall mandate. But there is a very easy test that can be applied to determine if either actually "leads" in their respective roles. Simply stated, it is *seeing what they do* (or don't do) when confronted with a situation requiring their leadership.

As mentioned earlier, is there *anyone* who believes that the schools are carrying out the wishes of the parents today? The policies that superintendents and principals support, those that their boards of education have established, are also those advocated and supported by their education coterie partners. Everyone is compliant! The only group of people *not* in virtual lockstep in their lockstep conformity is parents!

A middle school in the nation's capital is under siege. Teachers, parents, and students are in unison in complaining that their middle school is out of control. A dangerous gang, MS-13, routinely terrorizes everyone in the school. And while the evidence for their fear is abundantly apparent, their school officials deny that there is anything wrong! John White, a spokesman for the school system, wrote in an e-mail, "The principal is aware of concerns about gang activity in the community, but has not experienced any problems in school."[34] Writing about this issue for the *Washington Post* newspaper, reporter Michael E. Miller tells readers that the school principal, Rhonda Smiley, "declined repeated requests for an interview.[35]

As is apparent, the kind of leadership needed to resolve matters such as these, resolved so as to comport with the wishes of the parents, does not currently exist in the public schools. Those charged with leadership are not leading to this end. With this being the case in matters such as these, those entailing blatantly aberrant social behaviors, the expectation that leadership might be found in matters of instruction is a false one, especially when so many (the education coterie) are conformed to maintain systems that fail to produce results.

In the preceding pages, the education coterie was shown to be highly influential in maintaining the systems of public education currently in place. In the area of teacher evaluations, the coterie lends support and advocacy for practices found observably ineffective—those currently in common usage in the nation's public schools. In addition, the coterie has been instrumental in their support and advocacy for public schools teaching subjects that do not fall within the schools' educational purview. School principals must be vigilant to these incidences, noting them in the formal evaluations of their teachers.

In conclusion, if school principals are to reassume *true* leadership roles in their schools, whose function it is to assure that quality teaching is in place, a great deal of change will need to be engaged. The kind of leadership displayed by Mayor Giuliani, leadership based upon *knowing*, is the kind of leadership that must be engaged by school principals if teacher performance is to become better than it currently is.

Engaging that kind of leadership will call upon principals to step outside the protections their alignment with coterie-sanctioned positions afford them. To do such will require more courage than many most likely possess. As was mentioned earlier, it takes a *lot* of courage to confront the "you don't mess around with Jim" mentality that exists in the public schools today.

CLOSING COMMENTS

As stated in the preface, my intention in writing this book was to present what is, on the ground, happening in the public schools today with respect to teacher evaluation. In so doing, the school principal has been the central focus. This is *the* person responsible for assessing the quality of instruction, the *teaching* that is being done in the K-12 schools across the country. To show how the school principal came into the role of instructional leader, a brief history of public education in America became the starting point.

What the history shows is that when the position of *school principal* came into being, no one thought that it would come to incorporate *instructional leadership*. But with the passage of time, the position of school principal evolved into what it has become today, now centrally associated with *instructional leadership*. As a result, today's principals find themselves engaged in tasks that were not originally of their choosing, and are today beyond their levels of expertise. Educator and author Stephen Covey captures the context of this existent dilemma: "Leadership is a choice, not a position."[1]

Typically people seek work about which they believe they know enough to perform. But teachers, those aspiring to become principals, do not appear to be similarly motivated. When asked recently why she wanted to become a principal, one teacher said, "Well, I'm pretty good at organizing things and I have a few ideas that might be helpful."[2] The person asking the question, a university college of education professor, had this response to the teacher's answer: "There was modesty in her response and a sense that she did not have all the answers, but rather felt she could make a contribution. I'm glad I encouraged her to go for it, because she went on to become a successful school and district leader."[3]

These two people's statements represent a major problem in public education today: a lack of *knowing* for which *feeling* is substituted. This prospective principal gave no indication that she would need to *know* anything about instructional leadership. She thought her strengths were her *organizing* abilities and "a few ideas" that had occurred to her. And her professor was pleased with her response and "felt" that she'd be a good principal. And while virtually all the literature and commentary regarding school principals bespeaks their primary function as *instructional* leadership, neither made any mention of it.

While these two people cannot, statistically and/or study-wise, be presented as representing the totality of thinking in public education, their responses represent what is commonly found in public school education today. While instructional leadership is trumpeted as the principal's main job, it is not what principals do. As a sidebar, the professor referenced in this question-answer scenario wrote about the interaction presented here in an Association for Supervision and Curriculum Development (ASCD) publication. As was previously discussed, the education coterie, in this case acting in the form of the ASCD, continues to play an active role in maintaining the ineptitude, conformity, and obfuscation surrounding the issue of teacher evaluation.

The school principal's ineptitude in *instructional* leadership bleeds into *all* venues of performance wherein leadership is required. The paradigm of *leading* spans *all* venues of a principal's performance, thus providing the rationale for Mayor Giuliani's leadership experiences as germane to the school principal. As contrasted to those of school principals, what Mayor Giuliani's experiences show is that when people are expected to do things, they *must* possess the tools to do them! The kinds of tools and resources Mayor Giuliani drew upon are not in the possession of, nor are they available to, school principals.

Given the problems presented herein, those that lead to the definition of teacher evaluation as *fraud*, I've provided descriptions of some ways these problems might be overcome. However, while providing some suggested changes, I recognize that the changes presented may go unheeded, ignored by those in the *education coterie*. Most who inhabit this group exhibit an almost *palpable* inertial resistance to change as well as uniform (broadly conforming) refusal to acknowledge that a lack of *knowing* is even an issue for principals. And the higher up the pecking order one goes, from building principal up to the central office people, the more common the response "Principals know what good teaching *looks* like!" is heard.

If there is anything such as a "final analysis," it is this: Deficits in *knowing* prevent accurate and proper teacher evaluations in public schools today. Unless and until school people, those inhabiting the *education coterie* (interlocking school directorate) engage and deal with this reality, teachers will continue to teach their classes absent anyone *knowing* if they are teaching correct and proper information, and teaching it well.

A BIT *TOO* MUCH?

Some may have concluded that, in this discussion of instructional leadership, the matter of transgenderism was overemphasized, even perhaps in an overly critical, heavy-handed tone. But this issue was included in several sections of this narrative for a reason. The issue of failed leadership in the public schools is no better evidenced than by the distorted and contorted approach public education people take as regards the issue of transgenderism—superintendents and principals primarily. And while those in the education coterie are complicit in this failure of leadership, superintendents and principals form the front line in the protection of students. Parents expect them not only to educate their children, but also to protect them, as rightly they should. But superintendents and principals fail to do so.

Transgenderism, as it is currently being insinuated into the public schools by LGBT activists and others of their genre, represents the *greatest* challenge to public education in the 21st century. This construct invades virtually *all* provinces of the public schools: subject content, standards of acceptable social behavior, biological reality, and two thousand years of mankind's history, to identify but a few. Having the capacity to change the public schools, and through the schools an entire culture, this issue has been grossly mismanaged by those in the schools who are its leaders. In summary, these "leaders" have abandoned *true* leadership by virtue of their *ineptitude*, redefined their roles in *conformity* with their coterie colleagues, and engage in *obfuscation* to blur the differences.

With all the functions the public schools are expected to fulfill, learning in a safe environment ranks highly with parents. In recent years, the public schools have increasingly become engaged in what are called "social justice" issues. School "leaders," willingly relegated to becoming spectators, stand by and watch as special-interest activists seize both educational and social control of their schools from them. Their failure to provide leadership in instruction, *how* subjects are being taught, has now metastasized into a new and more dangerous area of their schools, *what* is being taught: the school's curriculum. They now fail to lead in both.

In years past, parents sent their children to the public schools with the expectation that what they taught their children at home would be reinforced in the schools. Parents expected that their schools would provide their children the *right and proper* learning and behavioral tools, those empowering them to do good things as well as become good citizens. Parents never expected, and rightly so, that their schools would be teaching their children that they were "privileged" due to the color of their skin, or that they could change from boys to girls, or vice versa. But the time wherein parents can maintain these expectations is over. With increasing frequency, too many parents are finding out that this kind of trust is no longer warranted.

IN CONCLUSION

International test-score comparisons have long showed that American schoolchildren are falling behind their counterparts in other developed countries. Added to this ongoing trend line of academic failure, American schools are now incorporating extreme sociocultural teaching, *proselytizing* children in matters that usurp the rights and responsibilities of their parents. *If* the public schools are to survive as the primary agents for educating America's young people, there must be a new awakening for those involved in public schooling. School officials, boards of education, and particularly *parents* must rekindle the need to *know* what's happening in their schools and then engage the necessary actions to assure that what *is* happening is what they *want to be* happening!

A PERSONAL NOTE

Humility, a prize to be sought and valued, is oftentimes difficult to maintain. Writing over two thousand years ago, Solomon cautioned: "Before destruction a man's heart is haughty, but humility comes before honor."[4] While stating what's *wrong* and what's *right* about teacher evaluation, writing *humbly* often seems to be an elusive target. Too much "I" creeps into the narrative, humility perhaps falling away as a result.

Based upon my time both as a teacher and principal, I've herein related my views about the practice of teacher evaluation and the lack of professional leadership in today's public schools. However, from time in the writing process, I had to smile as I recalled the words of Jack Nicholson's character, Edward Cole, in *The Bucket List.* In a scene from the film, Cole responds to a comment his personal assistant and valet, Thomas, addresses to him. Hearing what Thomas says to him, Cole gently pats the lapel on Thomas's neatly tailored suit and says, "Nobody cares what you think."[5]

If what I've commented upon here is helpful in changing what is, in my view, an ineffective means of evaluating teaching performance, that's a good thing! But then again, the words of Edward Cole might be the result. In either case, I hope that what I've offered can, at a minimum, result in more *open* and *honest* conversations about teacher evaluation and the leadership that *should* animate it. That would be a good thing as well.

NOTES

PREFACE

1. *More of the Best Stories of Bert Vincent*, Marion R. Mangrum, Brazos Press, 1970, page 31
2. *Leadership*, Rudolph W. Giuliani, Talk Miramax Books, Hyperion, 2002, page 195
3. *Webster's New Twentieth Century Dictionary of the English Language*, Second Edition, The Publisher's Guild, 1959, page 729
4. Aristotle, Quotes, Quotable Quote, https://www.goodreads.com/quotes/421677-to-lead-an-orchestra-you-must-turn-your-back-on

INTRODUCTION

1. Business Insider, http://www.businessinsider.com/pisa-worldwide-ranking-of-math-science-reading-skills-2016-12
2. https://quotefancy.com/quote/20445/Leonardo-da-Vinci-Learn-how-to-see-Realize-that-everything-connects-to-everything-else

1. THE WAY WE WERE

1. Protestant School Systems—Colonial and Nineteenth-Century Protestant Schooling, Early Twentieth-Century Protestant Schooling, page 1, http://education.stateuniversity.com/pages/2339/Protestant-School-Systems.html.

2. *History of America's Education* Part 3: Universities, Textbooks and Our Founders, page 2.

3. *New American*, October 18, 2012, Sam Blumenfeld, *Religion in Early American Education*, https://www.thenewamerican.com/reviews/opinion/item/13262-religion-in-early-american-education.

4. *History of America's Education* Part 3: op. cit., page 1.

5. John Adams Historical Society, The Official Website, John Adams Quotes on Education, www.John-Adams-heritage.com/quotes/.

6. *Teachers, Schools, and Society, The History of American Education*, http://highered.mheducation.com/sites/0072877723/student_view0/chapter8/index.html.

7. *11 Facts about the History of Education in America, The History of Education in the United States*, abcte.org/blog, https://www.americanboard.org/blog/11-facts-about-the-history-of-education-in-america/.

8. Monitorial system, education, Britannica.com, by the editors of Encyclopedia Britannica; alternative title, Lancasterian system, https://www.britannica.com/topic/monitorial-system.

9. Normal school, teacher education, Britannica.com, by the editors of Encyclopedia Britannica; alternative titles, teacher-training college, teachers' college, https://www.britannica.com/topic/normal-school.

10. Compulsory Education Laws: Background, FindLaw, http://www.findlaw.com/.

11. Protestant School Systems—Colonial and Nineteenth-Century Protestant Schooling, Early Twentieth-Century Protestant Schooling, op. cit., page 1.

12. *School Leadership through the Late Nineteenth Century*, 2013, State University of New York Press; Chapter One: Preceptors, Head Teachers, and Principal Teachers.

13. goodreads, https://goodreads.com/author/quotes/42738.John_Dewey.

14. John Dewey (1859–1952)—Experience and Reflective Thinking, Learning, School and Life, Democracy and Education, http://education.stateuniversity.com/pages/1914/Dewey-John-1859-1952.html.

15. goodreads, Leonardo da Vinci—Quotes—Quotable Quote, https://www.goodreads.com/quotes/679908-learn-how-to-see-realize-that-everything-connects-to-everything.

16. The 1900s Education: Overview, Encyclopedia.com.http://www.encyclopedia.com/social-sciences/culture-magazines/1900s-education-overview.

17. goodreads, https:/goodreads.com/author/quotes/485537.Frederick_Wilson_Taylor.

18. *Public School Administration*, Ellwood Cubberley, Houghton Mifflin, 1929, page 338.

19. *Effective Supervision: Supporting the Art and Science of Teaching*, Robert Marzano, Tony Frontier, David Livingston, Association for Supervision and Curriculum Development (ASCD), page 16.

20. Ibid., *Effective Supervision*, page 17.

21. The Madeline Hunter Model of Mastery Learning, https://www.doe.in.gov/sites/default/files/turnaround-principles/8-steps-effective-lesson-plan-design-madeline-hunter.pdf.

22. Madeline Hunter Lesson Plan Model—The Second Principle, Leslie Owen Wilson, Ed.D., page 5, https://thesecondprinciple.com/teaching-essentials/models-of-teaching/madeline-hunter-lesson-plan-model/.

23. *Educational Leadership*, February 1987, Association for Supervision and Curriculum Development, A Critique of Madeline Hunter's Teaching Model from Dewey's Perspective, Richard A. Gibboney.

24. *A Nation at Risk*, April 1983, https://www.ed.gov/pubs/NatAtRisk/risk.html.

25. Ibid., *A Nation at Risk*, page 1.

26. American Institutes for Research, October 30, 2013, *Three Decades of Education Reform: Are We Still "A Nation at Risk"? Two Steps Forward, Many More to Go*, Jennifer O'Day, AIR Institute Fellow, page 18, http://www.air.org/resource/three-decades-education-reform-are-we-still-nation-risk#Birman2.

27. Martin Gross, *The Conspiracy of Ignorance*, HarperCollins Publishers, 1999, page 249.

28. Alexis de Tocqueville—Facts & Summary—History.com, http://www.history.com/topics/alexis-de-tocqueville/print.

29. Alexis de Tocqueville and the Character of American Education, Dylan Pahman, Acton Institute Powerblog, November 21, 2012, http://blog.acton.org/archives/45852-alexis-de-tocqueville-and-the-character-of-american-education.html.

2. TEACHER CLASSROOM-EVALUATION: IS *THAT* ALL THERE IS?!

1. Boulder Valley School District Re2, 6500 Arapahoe Road, Boulder, Colorado, 80303, BVSD A-Z, Boulder Valley School District, Excellence and Equity, File: AC-ES, Confidential, Gender Support Plan, www.bvsd.org/Pages/default.aspx.

2. Ibid., Boulder Valley School District Re2.

3. Ibid., Boulder Valley School District Re2.

4. goodreads, John Dewey-Quotes.

5. *Paul Harvey's The Rest of the Story: 81 Astonishing Real-Life Revelations Behind Some of History's Greatest Mysteries*, Paul Harvey Jr., Bantam Books, 1997.

6. BrainyQuote, Sides Quotes, https://brainyquote.com/topics/sides.

7. *Scientific and Philosophical Perspectives in Neuroethics*, edited by James J. Giordano and Bert Gordijn, Cambridge University Press, 2010, page 13.

8. Ibid., *Scientific and Philosophical Perspectives in Neuroethics*, page 13.

9. Med Talking Points, Med News Views & Alerts, *Transgenderism of Children Is Child Abuse*, August 8, 2017, https://www.medtalkingpoints.com/transgenderism-children-child-abuse/.

10. "Public School LGBT Programs Don't Just Trample Parental Rights. They Also Put Kids at Risk," Walt Heyer, The Public Discourse, June 8, 2015, http://thepublicdiscourse.com/2015/06/15118/.

11. Prominent Psychiatrist: Transgenderism is "Emotional Unhappiness . . . Purely Psychological," by Michael W. Chapman, February 2, 2016, cnsnews.com, http://www.cnsnews.com/blog/michael-w-chapman/american-psychiatric-association-distinguished-fellow-transgender-emotional, pages 2, 3.

12. Josh McDowell and Bob Hostetler, *The New Tolerance*, Tyndale House Publishers, 1998, page 21.

13. Boulder Valley School District Re-2, 6500 Arapahoe Avenue, Boulder, Colorado, Boulder Valley School District Health Education and Community Resources, BVSD Health Education Approved Classroom Speakers, 2017-2018.

14. Boulder Valley School District Re-2, 6500 Arapahoe Avenue, Boulder, Colorado, Boulder File: AC-E3, Guidelines Regarding the Support of Students and Staff Who Are Transgender And/Or Gender Nonconforming, Names/Pronouns.

15. NASSP, National Association of Secondary School Principals, Transgender Students, Recommendations for School Leaders, https://nassp.org/who-we-are/board-of-directors/position-statements/transgender-students?SSO=true.

16. National Education Association, Safe Schools for Everyone: Gay, Lesbian, Bisexual, and Transgender Students, http://www.nea.org/tools/30420.htm.

17. Parents and Students Stand Up to Forced Gender Ideology in Schools, Breitbart Connect, November 24, 2017, https://www.breitbart.com/california/2017/11/24/parents-students-stand-forced-gender-ideology-schools/.

18. *Super-Charged Learning: How Wacky Thinking and Sports Psychology Make It Happen*, Richard J. Giordano, Rowman & Littlefield, 2015, page 43.

19. Parents in West Bend School District Upset about Survey at Badger School, Washington County Insider, by Judy Steffes, January 17, 2018, http://washingtoncountyinsider.com/parents-in-west-bend-school-district-upset-about-survey-at-badger-school/.

20. Video: Parents Air Disappointment to West Bend School Board about White Privilege Test, Washington County Insider, by Judy Steffes, January 17, 2018, http:/washingtoncountyinsider.com/video-parents-air-disappointment-to-west-bend-school-board-about-white-privilege-test/.

21. op. cit., Parents in West Bend School District Upset about Survey at Badger School.

22. Colorado Department of Education, 201 E Colfax Ave, Denver, CO 80203, Educator Effectiveness-Teacher State Model Evaluation System-Teacher Rubric, https://cde.state.co.us.

23. goodreads, Ernest Hemingway, Quotes, Quotable Quotes, https://goodreads.com/quotes/22956-the-most-essential-gift-for-a-good-writer-is-a.

24. Telephone interview, Monday, January 21, 2018, 4:15 p.m. EST, David Uelemen, Principal, Badger Middle School, West Bend Schools, 735 S. Main Street, West Bend, Wisconsin 53095.

25. The Widget Effect, Our National Failure to Acknowledge and Act on Differences in Teacher Effectiveness, TNTP (The New Teacher Project), June 8, 2009, https://tntp.org/publications/view/the-widget-effect-failure-to-act-on-differences-in-teacher-effectiveness.

3. THE WAY WE ARE

1. Bacow's Brains, University of California, April 2017, Lawrence Bacow on Higher Education, https://futureofcapitalism.com/2018/02/bacow-brains.

2. *The School Principal As Leader: Guiding Schools to Better Teaching and Learning*, The Wallace Foundation, January 2013, page 5, https://www.wallacefoundation.org/knowledge-center/Documents/The-School-Principal-as-Leader-Guiding-Schools-to-Better-Teaching-and-Learning-2nd-Ed.pdf.

3. "Should principals stop visiting classrooms?, *The Washington Post*, Valerie Strauss, January 8, 2014, http://www.washingtonpost.com/news/answer-sheet/wp/2014/10/08/Should-principals-stop-visiting-classrooms/?utm_term=.c05592771c01.

4. *Principal Time-Use and School Effectiveness*, Eileen Lai Horng, Daniel Klasik, and Susanna Loeb, Institute for Research on Education Policy, Stanford University, November 2009, page 9, https://web.stanford.edu/~sloeb/papers/Principal%20Time-Use%20%28revised%29.pdf.

5. *When Harry Became Sally: Responding to the Transgender Movement*, Ryan T. Anderson, Encounter Books, 2018.

6. Dozens of Children Disenrolled from School over Gender Presentations, The Heartland Institute, Cassidy Syftestad, November 7, 2017, https://www.heartland.org/news-opinion/news/schools-bans-parents-from-opting-kids-out-of-gender-identify-class-dozens-disenroll.

7. Becoming a Principal—Transition from Teaching to Administration, http://www.teaching-certification.com/becoming-a-school-principal.html.

8. *The Guardian*, Do you need to have been a teacher to be a head?, Nick Morrison, November 2012, https://www.theguardian.com/teacher-network/2012/nov/12/teaching-background-essential-headteacher.

9. "How Kat Cole went from Hooters Girl to president of Cinnabon by age 32," Entrepreneur Network, August 19, 2013, https://www.entrepreneur.com/article/227970.

10. Michigan State University, College of Education, Department of Educational Administration, Master's Degree Program in K-12 Educational Administration, Course Descriptions, 2011-12.

11. University of Northern Colorado, Greeley, Colorado, Educational Leadership & Policy Studies Project Course Schedule.

12. Ibid.

13. University of Colorado, Denver, Administrative and Policy Studies Master of Arts Degree, *MA requirements for students beginning the ALPS program in Fall 2016 or later*, Section C, Learning & Development or Diversity & Inclusion, SPED 5151 Slashing Stigmas: Promoting Positive Behaviors.

14. Washington State University, Fields of Study, Queer Studies, Department of Critical Culture, Gender, and Race Studies, https://admission.wsu.edu/academics/fos/Public/field.castle?id=41284.

15. ResearchGate, How many insect orders are there?, https://www.researchgate.net/post/How_many_insect_orders_are_there.

16. Science Alert, It's official: Your periodic table is now obsolete, 4 new elements have finally earned their spot, https://www.sciencealert.com/it-s-official-your-periodic-table-is-now-obsolete.

17. op. cit., U.S. students' academic achievement still lags their peers in many other countries.

18. Detroit worst in math, reading scores among big cities, Shawn D. Lewis, *Detroit News*, October 28, 2015, https://detroitnews.com/story/news/local/detroit-city/2015/10/28/national-assessment-educational-progress-detroit-math-reading-results/74718372/.

19. 65 Percent of Public School 8th Graders Not Proficient in Reading, Joe Crow, Newsmax, May 2, 2018, https://www.newsmax.com/newsfront/public-schools-education-reading-math/2018/05/02/id/857836/.

20. Detroit Public Schools Gave 8 of 10 Teachers Highest Ranking Despite Being Nation's Worst Urban District, Tom Gantert, May 6, 2015, https://www.michigancapitolconfidential.com/21275.

21. Robert J. Marzano, Daisy E. Arredondo, *Tactics for Thinking*, Teachers' Manual, Mid-Content Regional Educational Laboratory, 1986.

22. Ibid., *Tactics for Thinking*, Table of Contents.

23. Colorado Department of Education, State Model Evaluation System for Teachers, Teacher Rubric, https://www.cde.co.us/educatoreffectiveness/smes-teacher.

24. Ernst Haeckel (1834–1919), www.ucmp.berkeley.edu/history/haeckel.html.

25. op. cit., Colorado Department of Education, State Model Evaluation System for Teachers, Teacher Rubric.

26. Benjamin Carson, *Gifted Hands, The Ben Carson Story*, Zondervan, 1990, page 107.

27. YouTube, *Stand and Deliver* (1988/scene), https://www.youtube.com/watch?v=Q3a-bXXN9Xc.

28. op. cit., Colorado Department of Education, State Model Evaluation System for Teachers, Teacher Rubric, Element E.

29. Ibid., Colorado Department of Education, State Model Evaluation System for Teachers, Teacher Rubric.

30. *The Guardian*, Self-driving Uber kills Arizona woman in first fatal crash involving pedestrian, Sam Levis and Julia Carrie Wong in San Francisco, March 19, 2018, https://the guardian.com/technology/2018/mar/19/uber-self-driving-car-kills-woman-in-arizona-tempe.

31. ERIC, Educational Malpractice: The Concept, the Public, the Schools and the Courts, J. John Harris, III, David G. Carter, https://eric.ed.gov/?id=ED194963.

32. Coterie: https://en.oxforddictionaries.com/definition/coterie.

33. Cliffsnotes, 1984, George Orwell, "Critical Essays The Purpose of Newspeak," https://www.cliffsnotes.com/literature/n/1984/critical-essays/the-purpose-of-newspeak.

34. How to change people's minds: Attacking beliefs with facts never works. Instead, direct those beliefs to a different conclusion, Geoffrey James, Inc.com, September 2017, https://www.inc.com/geoffrey-james/how-to-change-peoples-minds.html.

35. op. cit., NASSP, National Association of Secondary School Principals, Transgender Students.

36. National Education Association, Legal Guidance on Transgender Student Rights, June 2016, https://www.nea.org/assets/docs/20184_Transgender%20Guide_v4.pdf.

37. Gender Spectrum, https://www.genderspectrum.org/quicklinks/understanding-gender/.

38. CHSAA Transgender Inclusion and Policy, Bylaw 300, Equity Code, https://www2.chsaa.org/home/pdf/transgenderprocedurepolicy.pdf.

39. *Educational Leadership*, The Schools Transgender Students Need, Ellen Kahn, November 2016, Volume 74, Number 3, Disrupting Inequity, pages 70–73, https://ascd.org/publications/educational-leadership/nov16/vol74/num03/The-Schools-Transgender-Students-Need.aspx.

40. Ellen Kahn, Human Rights Campaign, HRC Story, https://www.hrc.org/hrc-story/staff/ellen-kahn.

41. Wynne government targets "mother" and "father," *Toronto Sun*, October 16, 2016, http://torontosun.com/2016/10/16/wynne-government-targets-mother-and-father/wcm/6818234a-01cc-4b30-8712-37871eca5cef.

42. op. cit., Paul Harvey.

43. High rates of suicide and self-harm among transgender youth, Science Daily, August 31, 2016, Cincinnati Children's Hospital Medical Center, https://www.sciencedaily.com/releases/2016/08/160831110833.htm.

44. op. cit., *When Harry Became Sally*, page 48.

45. op. cit., *When Harry Became Sally*, page 48.

46. Anne P. Hass, Phillip L. Rodgers, and Jody Herman, Suicide Attempts among Transgender and Gender Non-Conforming Adults: Findings of the National Transgender Discrimination Survey, Williams Institute, UCLA School of Law, January 2014, https://williamsinstitute.law.ucla.edu/wp-content/uploads/AFSP-Williams-Suicide-Report-Final.pdf.

47. Public Discourse, Transgenderism: A Pathogenic Meme, Paul McHugh, June 10, 2015, http://www.thepublicdiscourse.com/2015/06/15145/

48. op. cit., *When Harry Became Sally*, page 91.

49. Press Release: UIL Statement regarding 2017 Wrestling State Tournament, February 22, 2017, https://www.uiltexas.org/press-releases/detail/uil-statement-regarding-2017-wrestling-tournament.

50. Gender Ideology Harms Children, American College of Pediatricians, September 2017, https://www.acpeds.org/the-college-speaks/position-statement/gender-ideology-harms-children.

51. Top Pediatrician: Transgender Ideology Is Child Abuse, *Church Militant*, July 18, 2017, https://www.churchmilitant.com/news/article/top-pediatrician-claiming-transitioning-children-is-child-abuse.

52. U.S. students' academic achievement still lags that of their peers in many other countries, Pew Research Center, February 15, 2017, http:/pewresearch.org/fact-tank/2017/02/15/u-s-students-internationally-math-science/.

53. Dr. D. James Kennedy, Coral Ridge Ministries, Fort Lauderdale, Florida, *A Godly Education*, April 27, 1986, https://webmail.centurylinl.net/h/print-message?id=20572&tz=American/Denver&xim=1.

54. Japan Might Be What Equality in Education Looks Like, *The Atlantic*, Alana Samuels, August 2, 2017, https://theatlantic.com/busines/archive/2017/08/japan-equal-education-shool-ost/535611/.

55. op. cit., *A Nation at Risk*, 1983.

56. University of Oregon, College of Education, Education Foundations major (BA/BS) https://education.uoregon.edu/program/educational-foundations.

57. University of Oregon, College of Education, Undergraduate Program of Study, Educational Foundations (B.A. or B.S.), 2017-2018, https://education.uoregon.edu/sites/default/files/2017edfprogramofstudy092017.pdf.

4. THE WAY WE CAN BE

1. op. cit., Paul Harvey's *The Rest of the Story*

2. "The Emperor's New Clothes," Hans Christian Andersen, https://americanliterature.com/author/hans-christian-andersen/short-story/the-emperors-new-clothes.

3. Lee Iacocca, Quotes, 50 quotes, https://www.successories.com/iquote/author/1269/lee-iacocca-quotes/1.

4. IMDb, *Magnum Force* (1973), Harry Callahan, www.imdb.com/title/tt0070355/quotes.

5. "There is no substitute for knowing!" Dr. Kenneth McFarland, Keynote Speaker, "Who Will Succeed in the 60's?" speech: Parke Davis & Company, First national sales meeting in its 94-year history, Cobo Hall, MI 1961, recording: "The Man in Salesman," Kenneth McFarland (Artist), Format: vinyl, Amazon.com.

6. Statistica, The Statistical Portal, 2017 ranking of leading United States chemical companies based on revenue (in billions U.S. dollars), https://www.statistica.com/statistics/257442/top-10-chemical-companies-worldwide-based-on-revenue/.

7. Relay/GSE, https://relay.edu.

8. Sposato School of Education, Match Education, www.sposatogse.org.

9. Sylvan Learning, https://sylvanlearning.com.

10. *The Economist*, Teaching the Teachers, Education Reform, July 11, 2016, https://www.economist.com/briefing/2016/06/11/teaching-the-teachers.

11. Garrison Keillor monologue, "A day in the life of Clarence Bunsen," Audio CD ISBN: 9780942110 388, 4/9/1990.

12. 9 Ways Japanese Schools Are Different from American Schools, Mental Floss, by Ellen Freeman, December 18, 2015, http://mentalfloss.com/article/64054/9-ways-japanese-schools-are-different-from-american-schools.

13. Ibid., 9 Ways Japanese Schools Are Different from American Schools.

14. Ibid., 9 ways Japanese Schools Are Different from American Schools.

15. 26 Office Etiquette Rules Every English Teacher in Japan Should Know, Japanese etiquette and customs that help you become part of the team, by Michael Richey, August 30, 2016, https://www.tofugu.com/japan/japanese-work-culture/.

16. Ibid., Parents in West Bend School district upset about survey at Badger School.

17. When Teaching Climate Change, Knowledge is Power, *Education Update*, May 2017, Volume 59, Number 5, Association for Supervision and Curriculum Development, Madeline Bodin, http://www.ascd.org/publications/newsletters/education-update/may17/vol59/num05/When-Teaching-Climate-Change,-Knowledge-Is-Power.aspx.

18. Ibid., When Teaching Climate Change.

19. Ibid.

20. Global Warming Petition Project, http://www.petitionproject.org/index.php.

21. Wall Street Window, The Students for a Democratic Society Goals and the Vietnam War in the 1960's, http://wallstreetwindow.com/students-for-a-democratic-society-and-the-vietnam-war.

22. Weather Underground, History & Militant Actions, Britannica.com, https://www.britannica.com/topic/Weathermen.

23. GLSEN, Day of Silence, https://www.glsen.org/day-silence.

24. Ibid., Wall Street Window.

25. *The Washington Post*, Next steps for student activists: More marches, walkouts and voting, https://www.washingtonpost.com/local/2018/live-updates/politics/march-for-our-lives/next-steps-for-student-activists-more-marches-walkouts-and-voting/?utm_term=.b8fd44692083.

26. Newsweek, Teacher Put on Leave After Organizing Walkout of Middle School Students, Maria Perez, March 27, 2018, http://www.newsweek.com/student-protest-walkout-ockley-green-middle-school-oregon-862579.

27. Master's Degree: Social Justice Education Concentration, UMass, https://www.umass.edu/education/departments/sd/social-justice-master.

28. Ibid., Master's Degree: Social Justice Education Concentration.

29. op. cit., *A Nation at Risk*, 1983.

30. UCLA, Social Sciences division, Gender Studies Courses, www.genderstudies.ucla.edu/content/courses.

31. *The Professors: The 101 Most Dangerous Academics in America*, David Horwitz, Regnery Publishing, 2006, page xliv.

32. EDJOIN, Job description-Los Angeles Unified School District, Human Resources Division, Class Description, Principal, Secondary School, https://www.edjoin.org/Home/JobDescriptions?id=32482jobType=certificted.

33. Day in the life of a principal, YouTube, https://www.youtube.com/watch?v=L7Cu6UrseSo.

34. Ibid., Day in the life of a principal, YouTube.

35. op. cit., Should Principals Stop Visiting Classrooms? *The Washington Post*.

36. *It's the Great Pumpkin, Charlie Brown*, Charlie Brown, Peanuts Wiki, FANDOM powered by Wikia, http://peanuts.wikia.com/wiki/It%27s_the_Great_Pumpkin,_Charlie_Brown.

37. Ibid., *It's the Great Pumpkin, Charlie Brown*.

38. The Holy Bible, New American Standard Bible, updated edition, copyright (most recent) 1977, The Lockman Foundation, Romans 5: 3–4, New Testament, page 199.

39. What Are the 4 Elements, Science Lesson: Earth, Water, Air, and Fire, https://learning-center.homesciencetools.com/article/four-elements-science/.

40. Quintessence, Definition of Quintessence by Merriam-Webster, https://www.merriam-webster.com/dictionary/quintessence.

41. Academy for Social-Emotional Learning in Schools, "The World Has Changed, Why Haven't Our Schools?" February 5, 2017, by Tara Laughlin, EdD (contributor), sel.cse.edu/the-world-has-changed-why-havent-our-schools/.

42. "What Is Student Engagement and Why Is It Important?" Jonathan Martin and Amanda Torres, National Association of Independent Schools, 2016, https://www.nais.org/Articles/Documents/Member/2016%20HSSSE%20Chapter-1.pdf.

43. *The New Toughness Training for Sports*, James E. Loehr, New York: Plume, 1995, page 7.

44. On the Similarities between Teaching and Selling, Charles M. Wallfisch, JSTOR, Vol. 9, No. 3, https://www.jstor.org/stable/41063279?seq=1#page_scan_tab_contents.

45. lizTheDeveloper, Teacher, Speaker, Leader, Mentor, Software Developer, "Teaching is Selling," January 16, 2015, http://lizthedeveloper.com/teaching-is-selling.

46. op. cit., Robert J. Marzano, Daisy E. Arredondo, *Tactics for Thinking*, Teacher's Manual.

47. Jack Malcolm, The Relationship between Selling and Teaching, http://jackmalcolm.com/2012/08/the-relationsip-between-selling-and-teaching/.

48. *The Guardian*, *"The Right Stuff*: Authenticity that's out of this world," Alex von Tunzelmann, July 2014, https://www.theguardian.com/film/2014/jul/02/the-right-stuff-reel-history.

49. Child Trends, Data Bank, "High School Dropout Rates: Indicators of Child and Youth Well-Being," Updated November 2015, https://www.childtrends.org/wpcontent/uploads/2015/11/01_Dropout-Rates.pdf.

50. op. cit., *Tactics for Thinking*.

51. Quote Investigator, Insanity Is Doing the Same Thing Over and Over Again and Expecting Different Results, https://quoteinvestigator.com/2017/03/23/same/.

5. LEADERSHIP IN PUBLIC EDUCATION

1. *The Worm in the Apple*, Peter Brimlow, HarperCollins, 2003, page 8.

2. *Leadership*, Rudolph W. Giuliani, Talk Miramax Books, 2002, page 100.

3. *Winning the Future*, Newt Gingrich, Regnery Publishing, 2005, page 171.

4. *The Death of Outrage*, William J. Bennett, The Free Press, 1998, page 129.

5. op. cit., Giuliani, page 227.

6. *American College Dictionary*, Random House, 1966, page 693.

7. op. cit., McFarland.

8. *The Conspiracy of Ignorance*, Martin L. Gross, HarperCollins, 1999, pages 13, 14.

9. *The Peter Principle*, Dr. Laurence J. Peter, William Morrow and Company, 1969.

10. *The Death of Truth*, Dennis McCallum, Xenos Christian Fellowship, 1996, page 105.

11. Ibid., page 123.

12. *What Great Principals Do Differently*, Todd Whitaker, Eye on Education, page 68.

13. Global Warming: Be Worried, Be Very Worried, *Time*, March 26, 2006.

14. *New Patterns of Management*, Rensis Likert, McGraw Hill, 1961.

15. *Theory Z: How American Management Can Meet the Japanese Challenge*, William Ouchi, 1981.

16. goodreads, James Bryant Conant, Quotes, Quotable Quotes, https://goodreads.com/15918-behold-the-turtle-he-makes-progress-only-when-he-sticks.

17. op. cit., *Leadership*, page 9.

18. op. cit., *A Nation At Risk: The Imperative for Educational Reform*, US Department of Education, 1963.

19. *What's Wrong with the World*, G. K. Chesterton, 1910, scanned by George Allaire, gall@globetrotter.net, page 56.

20. *The Schools We Need and Why We Don't Have Them*, E. D. Hirsch, Anchor Books, Random House, 1996, page 63.

21. Ibid., *The Schools We Need and Why We Don't Have Them*, page 63.

22. op. cit., *Parents and Students Stand Up to Forced Gender Ideology in Schools.*

23. op. cit., *The Schools We Need and Why We Don't Have Them.*

24. op. cit., *Leadership*, page 289.

25. op. cit., *The Worm in the Apple*, page 45.

26. *Slouching Towards Gomorrah*, Robert H. Bork, Regan Books/Harper-Collins, 1996, page 10.

27. Ibid., *Slouching Towards Gomorrah*, page 10.

28. BrainyQuote, Norman S. Schwarzkopf, https://www.brainyquote.com/quotes/norman_schwarzkopf_166117.

29. Bibleinfo.com, What is the background of the Ten Commandments, www.bibleinfo.com/en/questions/what-the-background-ten-commandments.

30. *The Ten Commandments: Still the Best Moral Code*, Dennis Prager, Regnery Publishing, 2015.

31. BrainyQuote, Edmund Burke Quotes, https://brainyquote.com/quotes/edmund_Burke_377528.

32. Newsmax, 2 Parents of Students Killed in Parkland Shooting Will Run for School Board, by Jeffrey Rodack, May 15, 2018, https://www.newsmax.com/PrintTemplate.Aspx/?nodeid=860342.

33. Ibid., Newsmax, 2 Parents of Students Killed in Parkland Shooting Will Run for School Board.

34. *The Washington Post*, "A ticking time bomb": MS-13 threatens a middle school, warn teachers, parents, students, by Michael E. Miller, June 11, 2018, https://www.washingtonpost.com/local/a-ticking-time-bomb-ms-13-threatens-a-middle-school-warn-teachers-parents-students/2018/06/11/7cfc7036-5a00-11e8-858f-12becb4d6067_story.html?utm_term=.d8b6e7b5f5ea.

35. Ibid., *The Washington Post*.

CLOSING COMMENTS

1. "Leadership is a choice, not a position," Stephen Covey, BrainyQuote, https://www.brainyquote.com/quotes/stephen_covey_636475.

2. "Why Do You Want to Be a School Leader?" Cathy Toll, PhD, University of Wisconsin, Oshkosh, http://inservice.ascd.org/why-do-you-want-to-be-a-school-leader/.

3. Ibid., "Why Do You Want to Be a School Leader?"

4. Solomon, Proverbs 18:12, https://www.openbible.info/topics/humility.

5. Scene from *The Bucket List*, YouTube, https://www.youtube.com/watch?r=BXRZ5c6l-vo.

ABOUT THE AUTHOR

Dr. Richard Giordano worked for over twenty-five years in public education as a teacher and secondary school principal. Having left the public schools, he developed a unique educational program to help university student-athletes maintain good academic grade-point averages while competing in sports. Beginning with football players at Indiana University and the University of Notre Dame, his "Making up Crap" learning heuristic was later employed to help both male and female athletes at other universities in a variety of sports. His work with student-athletes resulted in his first book, *Super-Charged Learning: How Wacky Thinking and Sports Psychology Make It Happen*, www.superchargedlearning.com. Dr. Giordano resides in Colorado. He is a frequent guest on the *Rush to Reason* radio show in Denver, speaking to the cultural and educational issues that impact the public schools in Colorado and around the country. He welcomes your comments about what he has written. Contact Dr. Giordano at drgioman@q.com.